# Sundays with Jesus

## Reflections for the Year of Luke

*James DiGiacomo, SJ*

D1003057

Paulist Press
New York/Mahwah, N.J.

Cover design by Sharyn Banks
Book design by Lynn Else

Library of Congress Cataloging-in-Publication Data

DiGiacomo, James.
    Sundays with Jesus : reflections for the year of Luke / James DiGiacomo.
      p. cm.
   Includes bibliographical references.
   ISBN 0-8091-4418-2 (alk. paper)
   1. Bible. N.T. Luke—Sermons. 2. Church year sermons. 3. Catholic Church—Sermons. 4. Sermons, American—21st century. 5. Catholic Church. Lectionary for Mass (U.S.). Year C. I. Title.
   BS2595.54.D54 2006
   252'.6—dc22

2006010354

Published by Paulist Press
997 Macarthur Boulevard
Mahwah, New Jersey 07430

www.paulistpress.com

Printed and bound in the
United States of America

# Contents

# Introduction

*Be doers of the word, and not hearers only (James 1:22).*

These reflections for the Sundays and the major feasts of the church year appear just as I delivered them at parish liturgies. They are offered as a resource for homilists looking for ideas and suggestions—but, more importantly, they are intended as devotional reading by anyone who wants to spend quality time with Jesus. The questions at the end of each may serve as starting points for your personal reflection or a group discussion. The content always derives from the gospel passages, together with frequent references to the other readings of the day.

You will notice that the reflections are not very long. This is because I am convinced that parish communities appreciate preaching that is not only enlightening and inspiring but also brief, clear, and to the point. Most parishioners do not care for rambling repetitiveness. These reflections aim at economy of language and richness of content. Whether they succeed or not is for the hearer or reader to judge.

Preachers who take their task seriously are always aware that they stand on the shoulders of others. None of us can remember all who contributed to our insights, but in this case special acknowledgment is owed to the commentaries of William Barclay, William Gleason, John Kavanaugh, Dennis Hamm, Dianne Bergant, and John R. Donahue. They all aimed at contributing to good preaching, and it is hoped that this volume will serve as evidence of their skill.

# Advent and the Christmas Season

Jer 33:14–16; 1 Thess 3:12—4:2; Luke 21:25–28, 34–36

*Stand erect and raise your heads....*

Today, the first Sunday of Advent, is the beginning of a new church year. It's hard for us to think of today as a new year beginning, because it's out of synch with other beginnings—the calendar year, the school year, the fiscal year, even the cycle of sports seasons. But then we remember what Advent is all about—waiting for, and getting ready for, the celebration of the greatest beginning of all—the coming of God among us in the person of Jesus Christ. In a few weeks Christmas will celebrate the first coming of Jesus two thousand years ago.

Today's readings build on the hope that the first Christmas brought to our world, and then urge us to look not at the past but to the future. Jesus describes that future in frightening terms that fit our own times all too well. He invokes the imagery of our primal fears. He tells of nations in anguish. Seas roar, waves crash upon us. People die of fright. This is a good description of our world today, beset by war and threats of war and the looming cloud of terrorism. Even the season seems in tune with this darkness: the days grow shorter, the nights lengthen, and winter begins.

But in the midst of doom, we are called to hope. Jeremiah lived in the shadow of looming national destruction, but he

1

reminds us of God's promise to his people that we will dwell secure. When Paul wrote the letter to the Thessalonians, he expected that the end of the world would happen in his lifetime, but he prays that the Lord will make us overflow with love for one another. Jesus tells us to stand up straight and raise our heads, for our ransom is near at hand.

It's not easy to be hopeful today. Just reading or listening to the news can tempt a person to despair. But during this holiday season, remember what it's really all about. Get past the shopping and the lists of greeting cards and the toys and the gifts, and remember that God is coming among us. In an unpredictable world, God assures us of his care. In the midst of our vulnerability, God comes as the most vulnerable of all, a newborn child. Stand erect and raise your heads. Your redemption is at hand.

*How do today's readings help you to deal with hopelessness and fear?*

## Second Sunday of Advent

Bar 5:1–9; Phil 1:4–6, 8–11; Luke 3:1–6

*I send my messenger ahead of you.*

On this second Sunday of Advent, as we look forward to Christmas, the readings all ring with joyous anticipation. The prophet Baruch says that we will soon see the glory of the Lord, the splendor of our God. St. Paul's letter to the Philippians is filled with promise: "I am confident of this, that the one who began a good work in you will continue to complete it until the day of Christ Jesus." In Luke's Gospel, John the Baptist proclaims the coming of Christ in the words of Isaiah the prophet:

"Prepare the way of the Lord.../...all flesh shall see the salvation of God."

So we're supposed to be happy and full of hope. But how is it possible? The world is in terrible shape. Every day brings news of more terror, death, and destruction. In the shadow of today's headlines, these messages sound hollow. But look more closely at these comforting words. When Baruch writes, Jerusalem has fallen and his people have been carried off into exile. Paul writes from prison. Luke's Gospel heightens this paradoxical affirmation of hope despite almost impossible odds. As John the Baptist announces Jesus' coming, Tiberius is emperor, Herod is tetrarch, Annas and Caiaphas are high priests. These men are the mighty and dangerous, the important and powerful people of the world. And who are against them? A desert preacher and an obscure carpenter from a town up north. Could the odds have been any worse?

Yet, look what has happened. The centuries have seen the rise and fall of great nations. The Caesars are gone; so are the procurators and tetrarchs and high priests, and they have left no mark. Who has survived? What reality was important? What word has lasted? Whose voice endures? It was the outsider, the baptizer, who addressed all history.

We cannot make light of the dangers and disasters that affect us today. But we must not let them defeat us either; we must not give in to despair. A light still shines in the darkness, and it comes from our God, the Word made flesh in the person of Jesus Christ. In a few weeks we will celebrate his coming and his enduring presence among us. With the psalmist we can say, "The Lord has done great things for us; we are filled with joy." It is not the joy of the lighthearted or the carefree—not in these terrible times; rather, it is the joy that comes from unshakable hope. The coming of Christ into the world assures that, somehow, in God's good time, "all flesh shall see the salvation of God."

*How can "keeping Christ in Christmas" help us to be heralds of hope?*

## Third Sunday of Advent

**Zeph 3:14–18a; Phil 4:4–7; Luke 3:10–18**

### *What should we do?*

Christmas is getting pretty close, and we're all making lists and checking them twice and figuring out: What do I still have to do? In today's gospel, John the Baptist has told the people that Christ is coming, and they ask: What should we do? He offers them some suggestions: Those of you who have more than you need—give to someone who doesn't have enough. Tax collectors—don't overcharge your clients. Soldiers—don't push people around or take advantage of them.

How about us? What should we do to prepare for the coming of Christ at Christmas? Advertisers have all kinds of suggestions to help us decide what to buy for presents. Here are a few suggestions for the next two weeks: Reach out to someone in need, and make their life a little better. Patch up a quarrel you've had with someone. If there's something in your life that doesn't belong there, put it at the top of your New Year's resolutions; or, better yet, try to go cold turkey. If there's something that isn't in your life and should be, try to make room for it. Apologize to someone you've hurt. Let someone who has hurt you know that they are forgiven. Cheer up someone who is grieving or lonely.

Last Sunday we heard John the Baptist tell us, "Prepare the way of the Lord!/…Every valley shall be filled/and every mountain and hill shall be made low./The winding roads shall be made straight,/and the rough ways made smooth." In these days leading up to Christmas, fill up a valley in your life. Level a mountain in your path. Make a crooked way straight. Make a rough way smooth. That's the way to put Christ back in Christmas.

*Name one mountain or valley in your life. How can addressing it help you get ready for Christmas?*

## Fourth Sunday of Advent

### Mic 5:1–4; Heb 10:5–10; Luke 1:39–45

*Blessed are you among women.*

The shopping spree is almost over now. We can catch our breath and reflect on what Christmas is all about. Even in the secularized version of Christmas that we are stuck with, many wonderful things happen: families are reunited, people reach out to help the poor, friendships are revived, and our world is brightened by acts of love and generosity. This morning we are reminded of what brought all this on. Christmas tells us that our God is not far off or remote. He is mysterious, yet as transparent as a child.

In the gospel reading, Elizabeth tells Mary that she is blessed not only because she is soon to be a mother, but because she has believed that God's word would come true. Beneath all the glitter and warmth of this festive season, a profound mystery is at work. But it can be perceived only with the eyes of faith. We look in the crib and see a God who loves us, not from a distance, but in our very midst, as one of us.

From now on, whatever life throws at us, Jesus has been there, for the highs and the lows. Have you experienced joy and success and a feeling of accomplishment? Jesus knows the feeling. Do you ever feel lonely or depressed or misunderstood? Jesus says, "Hey, I know what it's like." Have you known confusion or disappointment or failure? So has he. The Word was made flesh and pitched his tent among us. From now on, we are never alone.

This is an old story, told over and over, but it never gets stale. Christ's coming brings out the best in everyone—even those who don't believe in him! The commercialization of Christmas is unfortunate, but the gift-giving is appropriate. On this last Sunday of Advent, we await the coming of God's most spectacular gift—God's own Son. On Christmas day, when we are opening our presents, let us open our hearts wide to receive Christ the Lord.

*In what way do you believe that the promises made to you by God will be fulfilled?*

## Christmas

### Isa 52:7–10; Heb 1:1–6; John 1:1–18

*The Word became flesh and made his dwelling among us.*

These are the true stories of two men, a clergyman and a writer, who in very special ways help us to appreciate this joyful feast of Christmas.

The clergyman served an inner city parish in a very poor neighborhood. Many of his parishioners were homeless or living on public assistance. He wondered how he could minister to these people when his own life was orderly and comfortable. So, for a couple of weeks, he went underground. He lived on the streets, begged, ate at soup kitchens, and slept in shelters. Quite an adventure! It was hard, but he felt that if he was going to share the gospel with people, he had to share their life, too, at least for a little while.

The writer was the late George Plimpton, a well-known and respected author. Many years ago, as a young sportswriter, he wondered how he could write fairly and accurately about famous athletes and their exploits. What was it really like to compete in stressful and violent sports? So he sparred for a few rounds with Archie Moore, the reigning light heavyweight boxing champion. He participated in scrimmages with the Boston Celtics basketball team. He practiced with the Boston Bruins, played goalie, and faced hard pucks shot at him with lightning speed. He spent a week at the Detroit Lions' training camp playing quarterback, and wrote a best-selling book about his adventures, called *Paper Lion*. After that, he wrote about sports like someone who knew from experience. He had been there.

Today we celebrate the greatest adventure of them all. To show his love for us, God came all the way and became that most wonderful and vulnerable of creatures, a newborn child. "The Word became flesh/and made his dwelling among us." Like the clergyman and the writer, he had to find out what it was like to be a baby, a child, a teenager, an adult. Unlike the clergyman and the writer, he didn't stay for just a few weeks or a few plays. He was in it for the duration—for a lifetime. What a God we have!

When we look in the crib at Mary's child, we know that we are never alone. He knows, from experience, what it's like to be happy or sad or excited or afraid. Whatever happens to us, whether good or bad, God can now say, "Been there, done that. I know what it's like. I know how you feel." But he doesn't just offer sympathy. He brings salvation. "A savior has been born for us." It all starts today.

*Believing in Jesus as God makes it hard for some to imagine him actually going through everything we do. Why is that?*

## Holy Family

**Sir 3:2–7, 12–14; Col 3:12–21; Luke 2:41–52**

*And Jesus advanced in wisdom and age and favor.*

We sometimes feel so overwhelmed by all the bad news on radio and television and in the papers that we try not to think about it. But there is one kind of story that holds our attention and feeds our anxiety: a child is missing. Did she run away? Will they find her? Has he been kidnapped? Is he still alive? With each passing day we fear the worst, until suddenly one day the child turns up and is reunited with the parents, and millions of people who have been following the story breathe a collective sigh of relief. And even with this happy ending, it may not be quite over; there are questions to be answered.

That's what Mary and Joseph went through for three long days when, for no apparent reason, their son disappeared. It's a strange story that not only Mary and Joseph, but we also, do not quite understand. But it's worth thinking about, because the Holy Family's experience may be able to tell us something about our own families. Even if you're not married, or don't have children of your own, you know that raising a family brings with it all kinds of highs and lows. Kids make their parents proud and disappoint them, make them laugh and cry, make them worry and remind them to lighten up. To bring them up right, you have to play seemingly conflicting roles. You must be both demanding and reasonable. You have to challenge them even as you affirm them. You must know when to keep them on a short leash, and when to let go. And you have to do it differently for each kid. That's a big order!

Some parents manage by playing good cop/bad cop. Whatever works.

What was going on in twelve-year-old Jesus' mind when he dropped out of the caravan and decided to hang with the old scholars in the Temple? That's what Mary asked him, and his answer was not very enlightening. How much can we read into it? This was a young teenager doing what young teenagers do from time to time, acting thoughtlessly, without malice, following their instincts and neglecting to consider how other people might be affected. We are told that Mary kept wondering and turning over this strange event in her heart. As for Saint Joseph…well, on the way back to Nazareth, he must have explained to the boy why such behavior was unacceptable, and that he'd better not try it again, if he knew what was good for him.

Jesus, Mary, and Joseph were not plaster saints; they were real people, going through the same highs and lows that we experience. They remind us that, no matter what happens in a family, wounds are never too deep to heal. There were probably some neighbors who thought that Mary didn't do such a good job as a parent. After all, her son was executed as a criminal. That's how much they knew.

On this beautiful feast, let's thank God for the relationships that nourish us. And let's stick together.

*How does the Holy Family's experiences shed light on the relationships in your life?*

Num 6:22–27; Gal 4:4–7; Luke 2:16–21

*The shepherds...found Mary and Joseph,
and the infant lying in the manger.*

Today we honor Mary under her greatest title, Mother of God. There was a time when important people in the church wondered if we should call her that. Back in the fifth century, Nestorius, the patriarch archbishop of Constantinople, didn't think so. He put it this way: our mothers bring us into existence. How could Mary, a creature, bring God into existence? Was she greater than God? That would be idolatry. Instead, he thought we should say that Mary is the mother of Jesus' *human* nature, not of his divine nature.

In order to settle the question, they called a general church council at Ephesus. The church fathers decided that Nestorius meant well, but he was wrong. Jesus is one person, not two, and that person is both human and divine. Mary had a baby; and since that baby was God as well as man, she is rightly called the Mother of God. So, when we say the Hail Mary, we pray, "Holy Mary, Mother of God, pray for us sinners."

Nestorius was not the last one to raise questions. Some Protestants and other Christians have been uncomfortable with Catholics' devotion to Mary. They're afraid that she has overshadowed Jesus. But today, as we pay honor to her, we realize that it is from her son, Jesus, that she derives her special dignity. In honoring her we honor him. And because we are the Body of Christ, she is our mother, too. Just as we set aside a day in May to honor our mothers, we make this a Mother's Day for Mary, the Mother of God.

*What are your favorite images of Mary? What is her role in your personal piety?*

*How does the modern portrayal of Mary as a model for assertive, self-confident, contemporary women help you to live your faith?*

## Epiphany

### Isa 60:1–6; Eph 3:2–3a, 5–6; Matt 2:1–12

*We saw his star at its rising,
and have come to do him homage.*

What is God saying to us through this beautiful feast of the Epiphany, and what does it mean to us today? The way to find out is to see why Matthew told us this story of the Magi.

The first Christians, like Jesus, were all Jewish. As God's chosen people, they had been taught to keep themselves separate from the Gentiles. So when Gentiles wanted to join the early church, they didn't know what to do; it was a hard decision to make. St. Paul, in today's reading, assures them that "the Gentiles are coheirs, members of the same body, and copartners in the promise...." Matthew makes the same point in his own way. He tells of "magi from the east"— the non-Jewish world— coming to worship the newborn king. They have seen the light! The lesson is clear: Jesus is for *everybody*. At the end of his Gospel Matthew will have Jesus tell his disciples to go and teach *all* nations and baptize them. Don't leave anybody out. And that's how Christianity became a world religion preached to all peoples. But what does it have to say to us today?

In every age, we Christians have had to wrestle with a different problem. We know that salvation comes only through Jesus Christ, so what are we to think of those who do not believe in him? Down through history, there have been some who said that no one outside the Catholic Church could be saved, but the church has always rejected this error. We are taught and believe that there are many who belong to Christ without knowing him. They believe in his command to love God and their neighbor and try to live by it; and by his grace they are saved. They are children of God, our brothers and sisters.

At the last judgment, some of those who have fed the hungry and clothed the naked will be surprised to learn that what they did for the least of their brothers and sisters, they did for Jesus Christ. And they will be welcomed into his kingdom. These people live all around us. They belong to other churches, to synagogues or mosques; some belong to no church at all. (Some of them are even astrologers.) They try to live lives of justice and compassion, and they make better the world around them. Like the magi, they have chosen light rather than darkness. This does not mean that one religion is as good as another. It means that God so loves the world that he shines his light even on those we cannot reach. Today we celebrate that light, as we retell the story of the star that beckons to all the world.

*How do today's readings challenge me to be more tolerant toward people of other faiths?*

## Baptism of our Lord

Isa 42:1–4, 6–7; Acts 10:34–38; Luke 3:15–16, 21–22

*You are my beloved Son; with you I am well pleased.*

Today we celebrate the baptism of our Lord. The three readings all stress the same theme, that this is the beginning of a great mission. Jesus, filled with the Holy Spirit, begins his ministry of salvation.

Over the last few weeks, we have been celebrating Jesus' birthday and his childhood. Now he has come to manhood and is ready to begin his life's work. This work is described by Isaiah in the first reading. He will bring true justice to the nations—not by crying aloud in the streets, but by opening the eyes of the blind and freeing captives and those who live in darkness. In the second reading, Peter tells us that after John's preaching of baptism, "God anointed Jesus of Nazareth with the Holy Spirit and with power."

As we watch Jesus beginning his life's work, it's a good time to ask about our own lives. What do you think of as your life's work? What gives your life meaning? Where do you derive your deepest satisfaction? Some people define themselves by their work, by what they do during business hours. Some measure their success as human beings by the money they make and the things they own. Others get their greatest satisfaction from pleasure or fame or from the exercise of power.

All these things—work, ownership, consumption, pleasure, power—can be good, and often are. They're nice things to *have* but when they define us, when we find in them our whole sense of self, then we settle for being much less than we could be. We are made in the image and likeness of God, and God is love. We are most successful, as human beings, when we reach out to others in love—when we enrich the lives of others, when the welfare of another person means more to me than my own convenience. You and I are at our best not when we're achieving or owning or shopping, but when we're giving, especially when we're giving of ourselves.

The baptism of Jesus, which we celebrate today, was the beginning of great things for him. Our baptism was the beginning of great things for us, for it was nothing less than a call to greatness. In a little while, we will receive holy communion, the bread of life. That's where we get the strength to live up to it.

*How does my life's work fulfill my calling as a member of the body of Christ?*

# Lent and Holy Week

Joel 2:12–18; 2 Cor 5:20—6:2; Matt 6:1–6, 16–18

*"Return to me with your whole heart."*

Jesus tells us not to make a public display of our piety. Keep it between you and God, he says; don't spoil it by acting like a religious exhibitionist. So why are we walking around today with ashes on our foreheads?

In his day, Jesus was criticizing those who made a big show of their good deeds in order to impress people and earn their admiration. That's not what these ashes are about. On this first day of the holy season of Lent, we are being reminded of our mortality and the need to be straight with God and get our lives in order. That's not bragging; that's acknowledging our limitations. And if those who see our ashes are reminded of their own need, so much the better. We're all in this together.

*How does the imposition of ashes help you to approach the season of Lent?*

15

### Deut 25:4–10; Rom 10:8–13; Luke 4:1–13

*One does not live on bread alone.*

Jesus tells the devil that we do not live by bread alone. That's a good thought with which to begin the holy season of Lent. He uses the term *bread* not just to describe what we eat, but, in the way that has become popular in our time, it means "money" and all the things money can buy—food and drink, clothing, cars, TVs, computers, travel, appliances, and entertainment. Many people think that having enough of these things is the key to happiness—and the more money you have, the more you own, the happier you will be. There's some truth to this, but it's a very limited view of what goes into a meaningful human life. It completely ignores the human spirit—that part of us that yearns for something more than what money can buy. Many of the people who know this, whether they can put it into words or not, look to religion to satisfy this hunger. They go to churches and synagogues and mosques. They pray and worship and try to fan into flame that spark of the divine that lies deep within us. Our church sets aside these next several weeks as a special time to nourish that flame.

We Americans have a special need for a time like Lent. Our way of life can make it difficult to pay attention to our spiritual needs. There are so many bright, shiny things to distract us from what's most important. America is a consumer society. It defines the human person in terms of things owned and consumed. There's nothing wrong with owning and enjoying things; God wants us to enjoy the good things of the world he created. God doesn't want us to be poor, either. But he knows that shallowness and spiritual poverty are bad for us.

Possessions and pleasure and power are nice things to *have;* but when they define us, when they become the sum total of who we are, we become empty suits. This was the temptation that faced Jesus in the desert as he was poised to begin his life's work. How could he win the minds and hearts of those he had come to save? The devil laid out a program: get their attention, dazzle them with your power, use that power to give them material things. But Jesus had a different program, one that included service and suffering, one that led to a cross and beyond that, to the fullness of life. He resisted the devil; he remained true to his program; he was true to himself.

During Lent, we remember how Jesus went into the desert to pray and fast. In this season of prayer and penance and worship, we have a chance to get below the surface of our lives. What is God calling me to? How does he want me to relate to the people in my world? Is there something that doesn't belong? Is there something missing? Maybe I just need to be reminded how close God is, that God is always at my side, offering comfort and strength in hard times. In this special time of year, we have a chance to go within and, like Jesus, to find our best selves.

*How do prayer and worship help feed your spiritual hunger?*

*This year, how do you feel the need to go within, to find your best self?*

## Second Sunday of Lent

**Gen 15:5–12, 17–18; Phil 3:17—4:1; Luke 9:28b–36**

*This is my chosen Son; listen to him.*

Martin Luther King, Jr., in one of his great speeches, said, "I have been to the mountaintop." There, with God's help, he could see what most people could not—how America might become a nation where justice was available to all.

Peter, James, and John are on a mountaintop where, with God's help, they see with blinding clarity just who Jesus really is. Later these three men will see him at his low point, in the agony in the garden on Holy Thursday; but today they get a glimpse of what he will be like on Easter Sunday.

Years later, Peter will write to his fellow Christians: "We did not follow cleverly devised myths when we made known to you the power and coming of our Lord Jesus Christ, but we had been eyewitnesses of his majesty. For he received honor and glory from God the Father...[who said], 'This is my Son, my beloved, with whom I am well pleased.' We ourselves heard this voice come from heaven while we were with him on the holy mountain" (2 Pet 1:16–18).

Jesus gave his close friends a glimpse of his glory to help them through the hard times he knew were ahead for them. He still does this sometimes for us. Many of us have known peak moments when God seemed very real and close, and the spiritual world felt as real as the world of sight and sound and touch. It may be at a Mass when praying comes easily, when everything seems to fit. Or it may come in moments of quiet, when we're alone without being lonely. A sunset or a flower or a deserted beach can bring on those special times when we feel in touch with ourselves and with God.

These special moments are a blessing, but they're out of the ordinary. Most of the time we have to plod along without visions, without peak experiences, without even warm feelings. That's why following Christ is different from being in a parade. Palm Sunday was a one-shot spectacular, and so was the vision on the mountain. Most of the time we are like the apostles when they came back to earth; we look around and see nothing out of the ordinary. Only Jesus is there, beckoning us to follow him on rainy days as well as sunny ones. It's wonderful when we meet him on the mountaintop, but most of the action is down here in the valley.

*How do your peak experiences help you to sense the presence of God when you find yourself in the valley?*

## Third Sunday of Lent

Exod 3:1–8a, 13–15; 1 Cor 10:1–6, 10–12; Luke 13:1–9

*I have witnessed the affliction of my people in Egypt.*

A few years ago a rabbi wrote a best-seller, *When Bad Things Happen to Good People*. He helps his readers address a disturbing mystery that touches us all from time to time: If God loves us, why does he send us suffering? When tragedy strikes us and we're really hurting, we are tempted to cry out in anger against a God who torments us or just doesn't seem to care. "Where were you, God, when I really needed you?"

In Jesus' time, many of his fellow Jews believed that suffering was God's way of punishing sinners. They thought that if something bad happened to you, you must have done something wrong; it was your fault. That's the way they explained a recent tragic accident in which a tower had collapsed and killed many people. No, says Jesus, that's not the way it works. He understood the message of today's first reading, in which God tells Moses, "I have witnessed the affliction of my people in Egypt and have heard their cry of complaint….I know well what they are suffering. Therefore I have come down to rescue them." This is not a punishing God; this is a God who cares and comes to save.

This is a consoling truth, but it carries a warning, too. God will not force himself on us. In the second reading, St. Paul

19

reminds us what happened to some of the Israelites that God rescued from Egypt. Those who grumbled against him perished in the desert. Paul says: "These things happened to them as an example, and they have been written down as a warning to us....[W]hoever thinks he is standing secure should take care not to fall."

Jesus echoes this warning in his parable of the fig tree. A tree was drawing life and strength from the soil but was producing nothing. It was useless. There are two kinds of people in the world—those who take out more than they put in, and those who put in more than they take out. Jesus often reminds us that we will be judged according to the opportunities we have had. So it's fair for us to ask ourselves, "Of what use have you been in this world? What have you contributed to love and life?" We're expected to leave the world a little better than we found it. If we fail, the parable tells us that, like the disappointing tree, we can always count on God giving us a second chance. But if we refuse chance after chance, the day might come when all will be lost—not because God shut us out, but because we shut ourselves out.

So, why do bad things happen to good people? No one knows all the answers. But this we do know: God does not send the bad things. When misfortune overtakes us, we are not alone; God is with us, offering grace and strength. We are not supposed to be passive. Whatever happens to us, let's try to pass on things better than we found them, and leave the rest to a compassionate, loving God.

*How am I putting something into life, instead of just taking out?*

Josh 5:9a, 10–12; 2 Cor 5:17–21; Luke 15:1–3, 11–32

*This son of mine was dead, and has come to life again.*

There was once a judge in New York City who was notorious for his gentle treatment of criminals. His nickname was "Cut 'em loose Bruce." He inspired a character on a TV show known as "Let 'em go Joe." He aroused great indignation on the part of people who wanted strict justice. They could identify with the older brother in the parable of the prodigal son. Even the prodigal son himself agrees that he deserves to be treated harshly. He tells his father, "I no longer deserve to be called your son. Just give me a job." But Jesus tells us that God is not like that. He's a "Let 'em go God." He not only takes the boy back into the family; he throws a party!

God does not deny the reality of sin. He is not a sentimental old fool who closes his eyes to our shortcomings. He is saddened and indignant when he sees some of the things we do to one another. But he is much bigger than we would ever imagine. In this parable Jesus gives us an example of how to temper justice with mercy. He tells us to be ready to forgive, and not to be too insistent on calibrating the scales of justice.

The older son says, "Pop, look at all the money he threw away!"

The father says, "He's my son! He's your brother!"

This is a hard lesson to learn. But it's one that our world needs desperately to take to heart. In a world wracked by injustice, crime, terrorism, and war, there is so much righteous indignation! So many scores to settle! So much understandable desire to get even—to get revenge. There are real justice issues here. But peace will never come as long as people insist on 100 percent justice. Someone has to be willing to walk the extra mile. Someone is going to have to be ready to forgive. Without reconciliation, there can be no peace. And that goes for our private dealings with one another, as well.

Let's pray today that God give us a little bit of his great big heart. Ask for help to hate the sin and love the sinner—to overcome the natural urge for vengeance and go for the supernatural virtue of forgiveness. Like the older brother in the parable, we are rightly indignant at the way people waste their lives and the lives of others. But God reminds us: they're his children, our brothers and sisters. It's all in the family. Let 'em go.

*How can this parable help me when I find it hard to forgive someone?*

## Fifth Sunday of Lent

**Isa 43:16–21; Phil 3:8–14; John 8:1–11**

*Let the one among you who is without sin be the first to throw a stone.*

The scribes and Pharisees set a trap for Jesus. According to Jewish law, anyone who committed adultery should receive the death penalty, but the Roman authorities would not allow it. If Jesus agreed with the Jewish law, he would come into conflict with Roman law, and he would also lose his reputation for being kind and forgiving to sinners. If he said she should be spared, he would be accused of teaching people to break the law of Moses.

One thing about Jesus that you seldom hear is that while he brought out the best in some people, he brought out the worst in others. The scribes and Pharisees behaved very badly in this case. First, they were using religion to try to destroy a good man. Second, and worse, they were using the woman, treating her not as a person but as a thing, a pawn in a deadly game. Finally, they showed how vindictive they were. They enjoyed condemning people; they would rather punish than forgive. Their self-righteousness made no allowances for human weaknesses and offered the sinner no second chance.

These are the kind of people who give not only religion a bad name, but authority as well. Even civil authorities should be more anxious to reform wrongdoers than to punish them. This is why Jesus was a truly great religious leader. He had no illusions about people. He recognized their weakness, even their capacity for evil. But he never gave up on them. He always saw, even in the worst of sinners, the possibility to change and turn their lives around. So when he turned the tables on his enemies and made them walk away ashamed, it was a victory not only for him but for every human being who has ever repented and tried to start over. Now we know that our God never gives up on us; God's mercy fails only when we give up on ourselves.

There is one more important thing to notice in this story. We must not draw the wrong conclusion. When Jesus tells the woman, "I don't condemn you," he's not saying, "Don't worry, it's all right." He's not saying that sin doesn't matter, that adultery is no big deal. That's the way many people of our time think. Nowadays it's politically incorrect to tell people they're doing something wrong; they call it "imposing morality on others." The very word *sin* is considered outmoded, even quaint.

Jesus doesn't talk that way. He tells the woman, "[F]rom now on do not sin anymore." Stop what you've been doing, and change your ways. He doesn't pretend that all is well. He doesn't ignore the disorder in her life. But he sees in her possibilities that others and maybe even she has ignored. He presents her with a warning and a choice: you can go back to your old ways, or you can make a fresh start. It's up to you.

That's something to remember when we go seriously wrong or see others lose their way. God does not give up on us or on them; he is always ready to take us back.

*What can I learn from Jesus about how to confront the wrong-doing in my own life and in the lives of others?*

## Palm Sunday of the Lord's Passion

Isa 50:4–7; Phil 2:6–11; Luke 22:14—23:56

### *The Lord GOD is my help.*

When we recall what happened on Good Friday, the parade on Palm Sunday seems like an illusion. First the people hail Jesus as a king, and a few days later they call for his death.

Yet, despite the ignominy of the cross, Jesus was not disgraced; he knew he would not be put to shame. He trusted in God, and God was, indeed, his help. St. Paul quotes an early Christian hymn about Jesus' self-emptying and obedience to the point of death on a cross. For this ultimate sacrifice, God rewarded Jesus so that all creation should confess that Jesus is Lord.

No, the parade on Palm Sunday was no illusion. The crowds who greeted Jesus didn't know how right they were. This was indeed the king of glory, as we will see on Easter Sunday, when we celebrate his resurrection, his triumph over sin and death.

*Did any part of the account of the Passion, so familiar to us, affect you in a different or distinctive way?*

# Holy Thursday

Exod 12:1–8, 11–14; 1 Cor 11:23–26; John 13:1–15

*Do this in remembrance of me.*

Ask any Christian what happened on Holy Thursday, and the answer is, the Last Supper. And what do they remember about the Last Supper? Some will say, the institution of the sacrament of the Holy Eucharist. Others will remember the washing of the feet. The sacrament is recalled in Paul's letter to the Corinthians, the foot washing in John's Gospel account of the paschal supper. It seems at first as though our attention is divided between these two realities, but a closer look reveals a dynamic unity that is at the heart of the mystery of Christ.

When we hear Paul's account of Jesus sharing the bread and wine and calling them his body and blood, we are transported into the realm of mystery. When we contemplate the Real Presence of Christ in this sacrament, we know we are in touch with the divine in a stunningly intimate way. When we eat the bread and drink the cup, we are part of a sacred drama, proclaiming and making real the death of the Lord until he comes. This is religion at its most sublime, invoking the transcendence of God and bringing it down to earth in the symbolic sharing of a sacred meal. In this sacrament we come as close to heaven as we can on earth.

How different is the atmosphere of the scene in John's Gospel! This is about as down-to-earth as you can get. Dirty feet, covered with the dust of roads and sidewalks, leave their grime in washbasins. Hands get wet and dirty and wiped on soggy washcloths. No wonder Peter is offended at first. But this is a drama, too, and Jesus makes clear what it means: just as he has done, we are to wash one another's feet. How? By

25

reaching out to those in need, visiting the sick, comforting the afflicted, and working for justice. This is religion in the nitty-gritty. This is faith in action. This is getting our hands dirty in living out the gospel. How dirty? Well, one of the pairs of feet belonged to Judas, the man who had sold him out to his enemies. For a couple of years, Judas lived very close to Jesus. They traveled, ate, and slept in each other's company. They had shared secrets, confided in each other, gone through good times and bad together. Did Judas feel a twinge of shame at receiving this mark of deference from the master he had betrayed? Was Jesus making one last attempt to move that stony heart? We don't know. But we do know what Jesus is telling us: that the love of neighbor must go even this far—to forgive those who betray us.

The institution of the Eucharist and the washing of the feet are two sides of the same coin. So are worship and activism. The same goes for love of God and love of neighbor. They must go together. Otherwise, worship without a social conscience degenerates into religious formalism. And social activism without prayer and worship settles for second-rate secular humanism.

Tonight we remember Jesus' last words and deeds before he went to his death. This is his last will and testament. He leaves us with the Eucharist, his assurance that he will always be close to us. And in the washing of the feet, he tells us to stay close to one another.

*How do I integrate reverence and activism, the sublime and the nitty-gritty, in my attempt to lead the Christian life?*
*Do I ever feel as if I'm being asked to wash Judas' feet?*

# Good Friday

Isa 52:13—53:12; Heb 4:14–16; 5:7–9; John 18:1—19:42

*Bowing his head, he handed over the spirit.*

One summer when I was about ten years old, a tragic event made a deep impression on me. My family and I were staying at the beach when an eight-year-old boy fell off the end of a pier and was drowning. His older brother, who was fourteen, jumped in and tried to save him. While they were struggling in the water, some men saw what was happening and rushed out in a rowboat to rescue them. When they reached them, the older boy pushed his brother up and they took him into the boat. Then they reached down for the older boy, but he was gone.

When the younger brother grew up, he told his children about his older brother who gave his life that he and they might live. He's a grandfather now, and his children's children have heard the story many times. On the anniversary of the drowning and rescue, the whole family remembers and is grateful to the boy who, many years ago, gave his life for all of them.

Today we remember our older brother, Jesus Christ, who gave his life that we might live. It was he who told his disciples, "No one has greater love than this, to lay down one's life for one's friends" (John 15:13). On the cross, on the first Good Friday, he laid down his life for you and me. That is why, at this time every year, the church prays, "We adore you, O Christ, and we bless you; for by your holy cross you have redeemed the world."

We feel sad when we hear the story of how the boy drowned. But we also feel admiration for his unselfishness and courage. Good Friday is also a sad day, when we remember how the Son of God suffered so much because God loves us so much. But those two deaths, tragic as they were, were not unrelieved tragedies, for out of them came life. The younger boy, who was rescued, passed on life to his children and grandchildren. And from the death of Jesus comes the fullness of life for all who acknowledge him as Lord and Savior. The sign of that victory will dawn on Easter Sunday, when Christ conquers death once and for all. Until then, we walk the way of the cross with Jesus. Like that other family, we tell once again the story that never grows old of how "God so loved the world that he gave his only Son, so that everyone who believes in him might not perish but might have eternal life."

*What emotions do you experience on Good Friday?*

# Easter Season and Two Solemnities

Acts 10:34a, 37–43; Col 3:1–4; John 20:1–9
or Luke 24:1–12

*He is not here, but he has been raised.*

Today there are signs of life all around us. There are flowers around the altar. We have gone from violet to white vestments. All nature is waiting to burst into bloom. Christ has risen and lives again, and we all feel a bit more alive!

Easter is an affirmation of life in the face of death, a message of hope in the face of despair. We need it, because life is under assault today, from outside our society and from within. From outside, we have suffered the tragedy of 9/11. We live under the threat of terrorism. We have lost servicemen and women in Iraq. Within our society, there flourishes what Pope John Paul II called a culture of death. Abortion takes the lives of unborn children. A movement is under way to legalize assisted suicide and eventually euthanasia. At Princeton University, a prestigious professor advocates infanticide as his talented students take notes.

In the face of these threats from within and without, Christ's empty tomb tells us every year what we need to hear over and over: that sin and death do not have the last word, and that we should never lose hope. The disciples gave up on Good

Friday. They watched Jesus die, and they thought they saw the end of all their hopes and dreams. Giving up is something we are all, at some time, tempted to do, and some give in. Some people give up on church. Some give up on the government. Some give up on their families. Some give up on life, and some give up on themselves.

Years ago, there was a talented young basketball coach named Jimmy Valvano. His team won the national championship. At the height of his career, he was stricken with a fatal disease, and he knew it. He refused to be crushed. At a testimonial gathering in his honor, he made a speech that the sports fans among us have heard many times. In the finest moment of a young life cut short, he said, "Don't give up! Don't ever give up!"

That's the message of Easter. Christ has risen. Life has conquered death. Don't give up!

*How does my belief in the risen Christ help me to keep going in the face of discouragement and the temptation to despair?*

## Second Sunday of Easter

### Acts 5:12–16; Rev 1:9–11a, 12–13, 17–19; John 20:19–31

**Blessed are those who have not seen and have believed.**

Missouri is referred to as the "Show Me" state. It's the natives' way of saying, "I'm not gullible. I'm hard to fool." St. Thomas was like a man from Missouri. He had been burned once. He expected Jesus to head some sociopolitical movement, but it never happened. "Fool me once, shame on you; fool me twice, shame on me."

They say that seeing is believing, but is it? If you *see,* you don't have to believe. You *know!* Believing is a matter of faith.

Faith is a rich reality that includes taking something on the word of another. As the gospel writer says, "Blessed are those who have not seen and have believed." At Easter time, we celebrate Jesus' resurrection, his victory over sin and death. It is at the heart of our religion. St. Paul, in one of his letters, says that if Christ is not risen from the dead, then he has nothing to preach and we have nothing to believe. Most people find Easter too much to believe. To accept the good news, you have to make a leap of faith.

Faith is risky, because it's based on trust. We should be careful about whom we trust. But if we're *too* careful, if we play it *too* safe, if we always insist on covering all bases and being in control, then our lives can be narrow and constricting.

The greatest act of faith, for many people, is getting married. "For richer for poorer, for better for worse, 'til death do us part." Wow! Talk about taking a leap of faith! When we older folks are at a wedding, we know from experience how risky an enterprise the bride and groom are embarking upon. Who knows what joys, what sorrows, what consolations, what pain lie in store for them? But isn't it great that they are so trusting, so optimistic, so brave, in the face of so much uncertainty? Maybe this is why so many lovers today don't get married. They live together, they play house, but they keep their options open. It's understandable. They know how fragile a marriage can be, so they don't take a chance. They avoid the risks that come with commitment, and thus hope to escape the pain—what Hamlet calls "the thousand natural shocks that flesh is heir to." How much they miss! Only those who have had the courage to make promises and keep them have any idea.

Today we, the church, celebrate faith—faith in God, faith in Christ, faith in life. And faith in ourselves and in one another, because we know we are bought with the blood of Christ who will never betray our trust. We believe that Christ has died, that Christ has risen, that Christ will come again. So, with Thomas, we say to him, "My Lord and my God!"

*How does Thomas's journey from doubter to believer reflect your own experience with regard to God and other people?*

## Third Sunday of Easter

### Acts 5:27–32, 40b–41; Rev 5:11–14; John 21:1–19

### *We must obey God rather than men.*

In today's gospel, Jesus foretells Peter's death by crucifixion. In the second reading, we see what led up to it. Peter is ordered by the religious authorities not to preach Jesus. He replies, "We must obey God rather than men." He was reminding them of the first commandment: "I, the LORD, am your God....You shall not have other gods besides me" (Exod 20:2–3). To obey humans against God's will is the sin of idolatry.

Idolatry can take many forms. People may worship money or power or pleasure; it becomes worship when it takes first place in a person's life and outranks every other value. Sometimes the idol is some form of authority—a company or an institution or a government. Patriotism is a good quality, but when it is carried to an extreme it can be corrupted and become idolatry. During the Nuremberg trials after the Second World War, defendants admitted unspeakable war crimes. In their defense, they said they were patriots; they were following orders. They sounded a lot like our own Stephen Decatur, who said, "My country! May she always be in the right, but my country, right or wrong!" During the Vietnam War, at Mylai, an American officer supervised the execution of hundreds of unarmed old men, women, and children. In his defense, he said, "When I am given orders, I put the will of America above my conscience always. I am an American citizen."

This is the kind of thing that Peter refused to do. He was not the only one. During World War II, Franz Jaggerstatter, a young German Catholic, father of three children, refused to serve in Hitler's army. He was executed. Martin Luther King Jr. went to jail and risked his life rather than obey unjust racial laws. During the Vietnam War, Muhammad Ali and many other young men of conscience refused to fight, as a matter of principle, and the Catholic Church supported them. At the height of the Cold War, the American Catholic bishops declared that, while America had the right to possess nuclear weapons, it would never be right to use them. *The Wall Street Journal* called this "an astonishing challenge to the state."

People could and did disagree about these issues. But the principle is clear—obedience to God comes before all else, even one's country. Jaggerstatter understood that. Even citizenship and obedience to civil authority must yield. Doctor King knew that. This is what it means to say, "Jesus is Lord."

Most of us never have to make such dramatic, life-or-death decisions in obedience to the First Commandment. Let's hope we never have to. Meanwhile, we show where we stand by day-to-day fidelity to what we know is right, no matter what the cost.

*Where do you see the temptation to idolatry in your own life and in the lives of others? How do you deal with it?*

## Fourth Sunday of Easter

Acts 13:14, 43–52; Rev 7:9, 14b–17; John 10:27–30

*My sheep hear my voice; I know them, and they follow me.*

Today's readings are all about a party: who gets invited, who accepts the invitation, and what's in store for those who show up. The party is eternal life, the life that Jesus won for us by his death and resurrection, which we have been celebrating during this Easter time.

In the first reading, Paul and Barnabas are preaching the good news to a crowd of Jews and Gentiles, and offering life in Jesus' name. Their own people reject the offer, but among the Gentiles, "[a]ll who were destined for everlasting life came to believe" (Acts 13:48b). The second reading describes the fullness of that life beyond death: "[A] great multitude...from every nation, race, people, and tongue...stood before the throne.... They will not hunger or thirst anymore....For the Lamb who is in the center of the throne will shepherd them and lead them to springs of life-giving water, and God will wipe away every tear from their eyes." And who are these people? Jesus tells us, "My sheep hear my voice; I know them, and they follow me. I give them eternal life, and they shall never perish. No one can take them out of my hand."

When we hear of the party that Jesus calls eternal life, we tend to think of life *after* death. But we don't have to wait; it begins *now*. Elsewhere in John's Gospel, we read, "Whoever believes in the Son has eternal life" (John 3:36). Jesus himself says, "[W]hoever hears my word and believes...has passed from death to life" (John 5:24). Eternal life cannot be taken away by death but only by total and final rejection of God's grace; Jesus is himself resurrection and life. We're talking not just about how *long* this life will last, but about a *quality* of life. Whenever we see people living by faith, working for justice, and reaching out in love, we know that the party has already begun, and we are assured that it will never end.

Not everyone accepts this invitation to the fullness of life. But if we do, Jesus promises us three things:

1. He promises eternal life. If we accept him as Master and Lord, if we become members of his flock, our life on

earth will be enriched. It will share the magnificence of the very life of God.

2. He promises us a life that will never end. Death will be not the end, but the beginning of an existence beyond our wildest dreams.

3. He promises a life that is secure. Nothing can ever steal us away from him. We are subject to suffering and sorrow and death, but even in our darkest hour, we have his pledge that we will never be alone.

*Consider some of the ways in which your life has been enriched by following Christ.*

## Fifth Sunday of Easter

Acts 14:21–27; Rev 21:1–5a; John 13:31–33a, 34–35

*I give you a new commandment to love one another.*

Jesus tells us that we are to love one another. *Love.* Is there a word in our language more overworked, more misused? "I love you." "I love New York." "Don't you just love that dress?" "I love this game."

The Greeks saw the problem, so they have three different words for three different kinds of love. One is for friendship. Another is for erotic, sexual love. And one is the love that desires the welfare of the other and is willing to help make it happen. This last one is what Jesus is talking about. It's the one that sums up the commandments: "You shall love the Lord your God and your neighbor as yourself."

This kind of love is often accompanied by warm feelings, but not always. Sometimes it even goes against our feelings. It is the product not of emotion but of conviction and will. It's not the same as liking. We are called to love not only those we like but even those we dislike. We can't help the way we *feel* about people; we don't have control of our feelings. Some people are hard to like, and there's nothing we can do about it. Some people find *us* hard to like, even when it's neither their fault nor ours. We've all heard people say "I know it's wrong to feel this way, but…" No. Feelings are not right or wrong; they just *are*.

So the commandment that Jesus gives us is not to like but to love. He calls it a *new* commandment, but why? He certainly wasn't the first to tell us to love our neighbor; that was a basic part of the Jewish faith he grew up in. His commandment is new in two ways: he tells us to love not only our friends but also our enemies, and to love others the way *he* loves *us*. That's a big order! After all, he loved us enough to die for us. We find it difficult to love our friends that much. It's even harder to care about strangers. But our enemies? That's a stretch.

It may even seem unreasonable. But what does reason, enlightened by faith, tell us? That we are all children of God, sons and daughters of a loving Father. This makes us brothers and sisters; we're family. Watch the people in a courtroom where a hateful, guilty criminal is on trial. Everyone is against the criminal, right? Not quite. Not his family members who are in the front row. They know he's guilty and they hate what he did, but they don't hate *him*. They cannot; they're family.

Today we live in a violent world that is wracked by murderous hatred. We ourselves are the objects of that hatred, and terrorists commit one atrocity after another. We wonder when they will commit their next outrage. They are our enemies. How are we supposed to love them? We know that Jesus, on the cross, prayed for his enemies; can we? Are we supposed to close our eyes to the evil that is right in front of us? No, we can't, and we shouldn't. But we can try to hate the sin and still love the sinner; hate what they *do,* but not hate *them.* They're family. Like us, they have been made in the image of God, and

Jesus Christ died for them. Jesus says it plainly in the Sermon on the Mount, "[L]ove your enemies, and pray for those who persecute you, that you may be children of your heavenly Father" (Matt 5:44–45).

If you think you're not up to this, you're right. All by ourselves, we cannot love this way. But with God's grace, we can. If it were not so, God never would have asked us. During this Mass, let's ask for that grace. "Our Father, who art in heaven, forgive us our trespasses, as we forgive those who trespass against us."

*How do Jesus' teaching and example challenge the way I am relating to others?*

## Sixth Sunday of Easter

**Acts 15:1–2, 22–29; Rev 21:10–14, 22–23;
John 14:23–29**

### *The Holy Spirit will teach you everything.*

Some of you may remember, from several years ago, a very clever ad for *Levy's* rye bread. It was a picture of a young black child with a great big smile on his face, biting into a rye bread sandwich. The caption read: "You don't have to be Jewish to love *Levy's*."

Today's first reading, from the Acts of the Apostles, tells how the early church settled the first great controversy that almost tore it apart. The first Christians, like Jesus, were all Jewish. All their lives they had accepted, as God's will, certain traditional laws and customs. Males were to be circumcised, and all were forbidden to eat certain foods. What about Gentile converts? Were they obliged to obey these traditions? Some of the church leaders said yes; you couldn't change God's law. Paul spoke up for the Gentile converts and insisted that such burdens should not be imposed on them. It was a very difficult situation, a new problem for which there was no obvious solution. How could they change the law and still be faithful to a God-given tradition?

Well, they solved the problem and came to a decision. In effect, they decided that you didn't have to be Jewish in order to be a Christian. And the rest, as they say, is history. Christianity became a worldwide religion, open to all peoples. And what about their cherished traditions? They agreed with Paul that God was doing something new. He was calling them to go beyond the letter of the law, to remember what Jesus had taught—laws were made for people, not the other way around.

How were they able to do this? They said they were doing it under the guidance of the Holy Spirit. In today's gospel reading, Jesus tells the disciples at the Last Supper that after he is gone he will send the Holy Spirit to teach them all truth. When the early church grappled with the question of how to treat the Gentile converts, they appealed not merely to human reason but to the inspiration of the Spirit. They respected tradition, but they set greater store by the guidance of the Holy Spirit.

Jesus said that the Spirit would *teach* us. That means we must always be ready to learn. Being respectful of tradition does not mean having a closed mind. We must be ready to let God do something new. Sometimes that can be difficult. When the Second Vatican Council decided to celebrate the Mass in the vernacular and to make other changes in church life, many Catholics could not accept them. They said that some things just could not be changed. To this day they live in schism, convinced that only they are faithful to Christ, while we have betrayed him. What a tragedy!

Today we still have problems. Should priests be allowed to marry? Should women be ordained as priests? Should the teaching about homosexuals be changed? Is God calling us to something new? The only One who can tell us is the Holy Spirit. Let's hope that we listen.

*Where do you think the Spirit is trying to lead the church today?*

## Ascension

### Acts 1:1–11; Eph 1:17–23; Luke 24:46–53

*Why are you standing there looking at the sky?*

Remember Yuri Gagarin? He was a Russian astronaut, the first man into space. When he arrived back on earth, Nikita Khrushchev gave him a big bear hug, winked, and asked, "Did you see him?" That was quite a scene: two atheists making fun of religious people who think God is up in the sky somewhere.

Well, we know that God isn't "up" there. We do picture heaven that way, in our imagination. Sometimes when we pray we look up. At Christmas we think of God's Son coming down to us. But these are ways of speaking that no one takes literally. In the same way, we talk of "sunrise" and "sunset" even though we know that the sun isn't moving, *we* are. But back in the time of Christ, people did take such ideas literally. Everyone "knew" that the earth was flat and that the sun revolved around the earth. The world was like a big chocolate cake with three layers: God was up there, we were down here, and hell was down below. It's been centuries since people *thought* like that, but we still *talk* that way.

So what are we celebrating on this feast of the Ascension? Not a trip into the stratosphere, but the final triumph of Jesus and his entry into glory. For the last six Sundays, reading the gospels, we have seen the risen Jesus bodily present among his followers, showing them and us that he was really alive. But then it was time for him to leave them and return to his Father. How could they express this mystery? Only by portraying Jesus as going up, beyond their sight and into the heavens. Now he is with his Father; his victory over sin and death is complete. On Good Friday we pitied him; now we are happy for him.

And what does all this mean for us? The angels tell us, "Why are you standing around, looking at the sky? There's work to be done here on earth! We are to share our joy, bringing the good news to the whole world." Jesus says, "[Y]ou will be my witnesses...." He is not gone; he is with us forever.

Yuri Gagarin went higher up than anyone before him. But the cloud of unbelief prevented him from seeing what we can through the eyes of faith. The cosmonauts have conquered space, but the Son of God has conquered sin and death, and he invites us all to share his journey into everlasting life.

*What can I do to spread the good news?*

## Seventh Sunday of Easter

Acts 7:55–60; Rev 22:12–14, 16–17, 20; John 17:20–26

*I pray that you may all be one.*

In this gospel reading, which is taken from Jesus' prayer at the Last Supper, he makes two assertions that are both astounding and troubling. He says that his followers are to be one, and they are to convert the world. At first sight, it looks as though things haven't worked out that way at all. Christians are divided into many different churches: Roman Catholic, Episcopalian, Eastern Orthodox, and many different kinds of Protestants. Even the Catholic Church suffers from deep and painful divisions among our members. As for converting the world—well, we have a long way to go, to say the least.

That's the bad news. If you look more closely, though, you'll see a lot of good news, too. Yes, the Christian churches are separated from one another. We can never be happy about that, and never settle for it; we have to keep striving for reunion. Jesus himself wanted there to be "one flock and one shepherd." But let's not exaggerate our divisions. Remember what unites all these churches. They all acknowledge Jesus Christ as Lord and Savior; they share the same baptism; and they accept the same creed that we recite every Sunday. Whatever divides us is less than what unites us. They are our "separated brothers and sisters"—separated, yes, but still our brothers and sisters in the one household of the faith. Families sometimes break up, but the members never stop being family.

And what about that other prayer that Jesus made: his followers should convert the world? Well, we certainly have tried! And by "we" I don't mean just the Catholics. Those other Christian churches have always sent missionaries to all parts of the world and have won converts to faith in Christ. When Jesus was leaving this earth, he told his disciples to go teach all nations and baptize them. That effort still goes on. Young men and women among us still leave home to labor in distant lands, and you yourselves have always made generous contributions to their efforts. Those missionaries today see their work not only as making converts but also as working for the poor, ministering to the sick, and improving the lives of those whom they serve. These are things that must bring joy to the heart of God.

And what about the divisions within the Catholic Church itself? That's a sad story, and we have to try to do better and live in harmony and mutual respect. But, once again, let's not exaggerate. We Catholics disagree about a lot of things: birth control, women's ordination, homosexuality, capital punishment, and even war and peace. But we all come together on Sunday to hear God's word, to say the creed, and to receive Jesus

Christ in holy communion. That's a lot! It's a lot bigger than all our disagreements.

So let's keep working for Christian unity. Let's keep building bridges to one another. And let's keep bringing the gospel to people far away. All we can do is our best. The rest is up to God.

*How important is it for Christians to strive for unity? What can I contribute?*

## Pentecost

**Acts 2:1–11; 1 Cor 12:3b–7, 12–13; John 20:19–23**

### *Receive the Holy Spirit.*

What does it mean when we say we are filled with the Holy Spirit? It means that we are not just a group of pious, well-meaning people doing the best we can with what we have. We are the body of Christ, and the Holy Spirit is our vital principle, our soul. God is present in us in a special way, and we share in the very power of God. We, the church, live by the Spirit.

The church is more than an organization; it is a mystery. Because we are human, we are weak; because we share in God's own life, we are strong. We have the power to survive our own weaknesses, for this power is none other than the Spirit of God dwelling within us.

A casual observer looking in on us today sees only a group of ordinary people praying together—nothing out of the ordinary. He or she needs the eyes of faith to see deeper, to perceive that in this gathering God is at work in a marvelous way. We are ordinary people doing something most extraordinary, quite beyond the merely human.

We who have been baptized into the death and resurrection of Christ are a mixture of the divine and the human. The church has been through a bad time the past few years. The human side has come out in all its sinfulness, shocking those outside and shaming us within. But the same Jesus who told us there would be scandals also told us he would send us an Advocate, the Spirit of Truth. This Spirit was given to us at our baptism and confirmation.

The disciples who received the Spirit on the first Pentecost did marvelous things. In less spectacular ways, so can we. The Spirit is at work within us when instead of being selfish, we are generous; when instead of holding grudges, we are reconciled with those who offend us; when instead of cutting corners, we act with integrity; when instead of being cruel, we are gentle and kind; when we are tempted to act out of anger and instead try to be patient; when we confront our prejudices and give everyone the respect they deserve; when, in the face of a culture of death, we stand up for life.

Today the world is in bad shape. It would be a lot worse if the Spirit did not do these extraordinary good things through ordinary people like us. On this great feast of Pentecost, we celebrate the presence of the Spirit working through us for a better world.

*Can I perceive the Spirit working in the church despite its obvious imperfections?*

## Trinity Sunday

**Prov 8:22–31; Rom 5:1–5; John 16:12–15**

*Glory to the Father, the Son and the Holy Spirit.*

When Jesus was a little boy, his mother taught him his prayers. On getting up in the morning, he learned to say the Shema: "Hear, O Israel, the Lord is our God, the Lord is One" (cf. Deut 6:4). But when we bless ourselves, we say, "In the name of the Father and the Son and the Holy Spirit." God sounds like three. Indeed, Jews and Muslims, who worship the same God as we, have wondered if we Christians have one God or three. Why do we insist on addressing God as Three in One? Because that is the way Jesus has revealed him.

When he was on earth, Jesus called God his Father: "Everything that the Father has is mine." Then he promised to send the Spirit: "When he comes, the Spirit of truth, he will guide you to all truth."

St. Paul tells us, "We have peace with God through our Lord Jesus Christ" and that "the love of God has been poured out into our hearts through the Holy Spirit that has been given to us." We are not only a chosen people, we are children of God. Indeed, we are the very body of Christ, and the Holy Spirit is our soul.

The more we try to grasp this God, the more we realize that he is utterly beyond our comprehension. And yet, paradoxically, he is so close to us in Jesus, who pitched his tent among us and became truly one of us. On this feast of the Holy Trinity, we celebrate the richness, the awesome mysteriousness of our God. We praise him for his majesty, we revel in his goodness, we thank him for his loving care.

Mysteries are not like puzzles. Puzzles are meant to be solved. Mysteries are meant to be contemplated, pondered, wondered at, and proclaimed. The mystery of the Trinity not only tells us who God is, it gives us a glimpse of who we are and what we are meant to be: "children of God, and if children, then heirs, heirs of God and joint heirs with Christ" (Rom 8:16–17). Until then, we try to carry out his final command to "make disciples of all nations, baptizing them in the name of the Father, and of the Son, and of the holy Spirit" (Matt 28:19).

*How is belief in the Trinity reflected in my piety and in the prayer of the church?*

## The Body and Blood of Christ

Gen 14:18–20; 1 Cor 11:23–26; Luke 9:11b–17

*This is my body that is for you.*

If you go to an art museum and look at oil paintings, you must not stand too close. To get the proper perspective, you have to step back. Today's feast of the body and blood of Christ is like that. It's a great mystery, and we're so close to it that once a year we step back in order to see it more clearly.

There are two main aspects to this mystery—the real presence and the bread of life.

*The real presence.* Since Jesus Christ is truly present in the consecrated bread and wine, we respond with an attitude of *reverence*. Over the centuries, this reverence has been expressed in various ways that have changed from time to time. In Catholic countries there were outdoor processions in which the consecrated host was displayed. In Texas, the city of Corpus Christi gets its name from this feast. Benediction of the blessed sacrament and forty hours devotion have been popular expressions of adoration. Kneeling is one way of expressing reverence. Some of us remember when only the priest was allowed to touch the consecrated host and communion could be received only on the tongue. In the Middle Ages this attitude was so strong that many people expressed their reverence by not receiving communion! That's why the church had to make it a law that Catholics must receive communion at least once a year. Such distortions came about because people had lost sight of the other dimension of this mystery—the bread of life.

*The bread of life.* This dimension is the one expressed in the gospel reading, in which Jesus feeds the crowd with a few loaves of bread. This act recalled how God fed the Israelites in the desert, and it foreshadowed the feeding of us in the Eucharist. Some of us are old enough to remember when many devout Catholics did not receive at Mass; communion was considered something "extra." We worshiped Jesus in the Eucharist, but we forgot that bread and wine are food and drink, meant to be our nourishment. I grew up thinking that you shouldn't go to communion unless you went to confession first. Now we realize that the only reason for not receiving is having an unconfessed mortal sin. During and after the Second Vatican Council the church recovered this meal aspect of the Mass. New customs grew up. We now had the option of receiving communion in the hand and of drinking from the chalice. Lay people, as well as priests, could distribute communion. Not everyone was comfortable with these new ways, so we are given a choice.

All these historical developments and fluctuations reflect the attempts of God's people to relate to a great mystery. It is one of astounding intimacy. God so wants to be close to us that his Son gives himself to us under the humble appearances of bread and wine. In a few minutes we will honor the request made at the Last Supper to remember him, and we will respond to his invitation to take and eat. This is food for the journey, nourishment for the spirit, strength to deal with whatever life throws at us.

*Which aspect of the Eucharist—real presence or bread of life—is more meaningful to you? Why?*

# Ordinary Time

Isa 62:1–5; 1 Cor 12:4–11; John 2:1–11

### *They have no wine.*

It's interesting to observe the way Mary acts during the wedding feast at Cana. She is worried that the wine may run out; in the Jewish society of her day, that would have been a great embarrassment for the newlyweds and their families. She turns to her Son and expresses her concern in a simple, direct way: "They have no wine." Jesus doesn't give her any encouragement; he indicates that it's not his problem: "Woman, how does your concern affect me?" He says his hour has not yet come: was he on some kind of schedule? But she doesn't give up; she goes to the waiters and tells them, "Do whatever he tells you." What's going on here?

It looks as though Mary was a widow by this time. The gospels never mention Joseph during the accounts of Jesus' adult years. At the age of thirty, he is still living with his mother; she probably needed him to support her. She knows her Son very well. So, even when he seems to refuse her request, she tells the servers to do whatever he says. She has the kind of faith that trusts even when it does not understand. She didn't know what he would do, but she trusted him to do the right thing. And he did!

47

We have all known times in our lives when we didn't know what to do. Things happen to us that make no sense, and we can't find our way. That's when we need the kind of faith that Mary had—the faith that enables us to trust even when we don't understand. In times of trouble and confusion, we can turn to Jesus even when it looks as though he can't do anything or doesn't want to. Mary knew him better than that, and so should we. He never let her down, and he feels the same way about us.

*Watching Mary and Jesus interact, what insight do I get into my own relationship with each of them?*

## Third Sunday of the Year

Neh 8:2–4a, 5–6, 8–10; 1 Cor 12:12–30;
Luke 1:1–4; 4:14–21

*Today this Scripture passage is fulfilled in your hearing.*

Jesus says that he has come to bring glad tidings to the poor, freedom to captives, sight to the blind, and release of prisoners. The people who heard him were citizens of an occupied country living under a brutal, oppressive Roman regime. Some thought he was preaching armed revolution, but he had a different kind of revolution in mind. He knew that people have to change inside before they can change things around them. So he tells them, and us, that before we try to change the world, we have to change ourselves.

He tells them not just in words but also by dramatic, unforgettable deeds. He cures a blind man as a sign that he can cure our blindness. He can help us to see what's really important and how to live. He casts out demons to show us that we, too, can be free of the demons within ourselves—our selfishness, our greed, our anger, our resentments, our infidelities. He raises the dead to show that a fuller life is available to us. The world cannot be just and loving until we individual men and women are just and loving. But that's not the whole of Jesus' message. Christianity is not an individualistic, exclusively spiritual religion that looks only to the salvation of individual souls. God cares about us not only individually but as a people and about our way of life.

How does God see us as a people?
What does he think of our society?
What judgment does he pass on our way of life?

Our nation has poor people in abundance. That's not news; every country has always had its poor. But in America, the poor are surrounded by obscene wealth and wastefulness practiced by a privileged few. Social justice in this country is still a long way off. There is blindness all around us, in the form of false values, sexual irresponsibility, and disrespect for life. Many of our fellow citizens are oppressed—deprived of opportunities for employment, lacking medical insurance, bearing unfair tax burdens, treated as second class citizens because of their sex or race or national origin. All of this in a land where there would be enough for everyone if only we were willing to share.

When we think of all these inequities, Jesus' proclamation of salvation can sound pretty hollow, like wishful thinking, just as they sounded to the people of Nazareth struggling under Roman domination. And yet, in the face of these discouraging realities, Jesus tells them and you and me that it does not have to be this way. No matter how far away God may seem, he is with us, working within us. With God's help we can change ourselves for the better. And we can make the world around us a little more loving and just by the way we work, spend, vote, and love. That's the challenge, and the source of our hope. That's the good news of salvation in Jesus Christ.

*Are there any ways in which I might change things for the better, beginning with myself?*

## Fourth Sunday of the Year

Jer 1:4–5, 17–19; 1 Cor 12:31—13:13; Luke 4:21–30

*No prophet is accepted in his own native place.*

When local boys and girls become famous, the town celebrates them by having a parade in their honor. But Jesus' return to Nazareth was a public relations disaster, for two reasons: he was too familiar to them, and he refused to be as provincial and narrow-minded as they were. He came back to his hometown with a reputation for having done great things elsewhere. When he started to speak, they were impressed. But then someone broke the spell: "We know him; he can't be much." And things got worse when Jesus reminded them how ancient prophets had been sent by God to the Gentiles. Some of Jesus' neighbors were convinced that if the Jews were God's chosen people, then God must despise everyone else. Yet, here was the young Jesus telling them that Gentiles were loved by God. This was something new, and they didn't come to the synagogue to hear something new.

The people of Nazareth came to the synagogue to pray and to hear the word of God. They would listen to rabbis as long as they offered no new ideas; they didn't want any surprises. Their idea of God was a domesticated deity who was not supposed to shake them out of their complacency. When Jesus refused to reinforce their prejudices, they violently rejected him.

Jesus was not the last religious leader to meet this kind of opposition. Most people who go to synagogues or mosques or churches want to be comforted and consoled. We enjoy familiar ritual, we feel affirmed in our values and strengthened in our convictions. When we are challenged to think of God and Jesus in new ways, to embrace new styles of prayer and worship, to reach out to non-Catholics, and to accept new ways of dealing with sex and gender, it can be threatening. Our church has been seriously divided over these matters for the last forty years. Not everything new is necessarily good. Changes in the church have to be carefully scrutinized and evaluated. But sometimes God calls us to leave the safety of the past and to set out for parts unknown. God never gives up on us and is always ready to help us do better.

Several years ago the Holiday Inn motel chain ran an advertising campaign. Its motto was "no surprises." They promised that your room and service would be just like last time, with no unexpected features to disturb you. The church is not Holiday Inn. It is the house of God. We offer comfort and encouragement, but we can't guarantee that there will never be any surprises. The God of Jesus Christ is too big to be limited by our expectations. He challenges us, and he guarantees the grace to meet those challenges. That's because he believes in us, even more than we believe in ourselves.

*How am I called by my faith and my church to be part of something new?*

## Fifth Sunday of the Year

Isa 6:1–2a, 3–8; 1 Cor 15:1–11; Luke 5:1–11

*Do not be afraid; from now on you will be catching men.*

People in business know that you have to spend money to make money. If you don't take risks, you don't succeed. If you play it too safe, opportunity passes you by. This is true not only in business but in life itself and in our dealings with God. When Jesus tells them to cast the nets, Peter thinks to himself, *This Jesus is a good carpenter and a great preacher, but he doesn't know fishing. We found out last night that this is the wrong place at the wrong time. The nets are big and heavy, and the men are tired.* The down-to-earth realist in Peter says: "Forget it." But the other side of Peter—the dreamer, the adventurer—says: "Why not? You never can tell what may happen." So Peter and his men take a chance, and they strike it rich.

Jesus worked a miracle that day because Peter let him. Peter trusted Jesus and took a chance. If Peter hadn't opened himself up to a new experience, nothing would have happened. All sorts of possibilities in him might never have been realized, and history would never have heard of a few Galilean fishermen in an obscure town. The spirit of trust and adventure made all the difference. It was always this way with Jesus. Over and over again in the gospels, when the blind and the lame and the sick were cured, he told them their faith had made them whole. When people closed themselves off through skepticism or fear, he could not do anything for them. This sort of thing still goes on today. Many lovers play it safe; they're afraid to pledge themselves in marriage. Others believe in each other enough to plunge into the deep—for richer for poorer, for better or worse, 'til death do them part—and they are not alone, for God is with them.

When the Galilean fishermen finished scrambling and emptied the nets on shore, it dawned on them that they were in the presence of a mysterious, awesome power, and they were afraid. Peter cries out, "Depart from me, Lord, for I am a sinful man." He sounds like Isaiah in the first reading: "Woe is me! … I am a man of unclean lips; yet my eyes have seen the King, the LORD of hosts!" This is the way people sometimes feel about God. They are so aware of their shortcomings, they can't imagine God wanting to have anything to do with them. To Peter, and to everyone who has ever felt this way, Jesus says, "Do not be afraid." This catch of fish is nothing compared to what you will do later.

So it's all about trusting and taking risks. Anyone who seriously tries to follow Jesus Christ knows that it isn't easy. Most people think it costs too much. Peter and his men know better, and so do we. As St. Paul tells us, this is what we preach, and this is what we believe.

*How may God be calling me to take a leap of faith?*

## *Sixth Sunday of the Year*

Jer 17:5–8; 1 Cor 15:12, 16–20; Luke 6:17, 20–26

### *Your reward will be great in heaven.*

If I asked you: Would you rather be rich or poor? laugh or cry? have a full stomach or an empty one? be well thought of, or have a bad reputation? You know what you would say. Most of us agree with the man who said: "I've been rich and I've been poor, and, believe me, rich is better." So what is Jesus talking about? He's not saying that if you're unhappy now you'll be happy in heaven. It's not that simple.

There is no evil in riches or contentment or comfort. Morally speaking, they are neither good nor bad. The same goes for poverty, grief, and suffering; they are no guarantee of virtue. There have been rich saints and poor villains. The problem with riches is that they are a temptation. They can lull us into a false sense of self-sufficiency, so that we think we don't need anybody, including God. Archbishop Romero, the martyred bishop of El Salvador, said, "Woe to anyone who touches wealth; it is like a high-tension wire that burns you." The same goes for suffering. Two of the great heroes of our time, Martin Luther King, Jr. and Jackie Robinson, were ennobled by trials and suffering. Otherwise, they probably would have led relatively undistinguished lives.

Look back on your own life. What are you most proud of? What did suffering and trials do for you? You probably know, from experience, the wisdom of that saying: "Don't pray for an easy life. Pray to be a strong person." There is a parallel in the experience of being parents. Parents who bring up children denying them nothing and never challenging them sell them short. Does God, then, send us trials and suffering to test us? No. These things come our way without God having anything to do with them. But the way we deal with them has much to do with the kind of persons we become. Jesus assures us that there is more to life than making a living, more than a full stomach, more than a comfortable lifestyle. When we look at our own lives and the lives of those we admire, we know he's right. What may have seemed like an outrageous, nonsensical comment on the human condition is actually a profound insight into what makes a good human being.

So keep working hard, make as much money as you can, try to be comfortable and secure. It's okay. Just remember what Jesus says is the bottom line. Don't put your complete trust in anything less than God himself. In the long run, nothing less than God will ever satisfy you.

*Are there ways in which hard times and trials have made me a stronger person?*

1 Sam 26: 2, 7–9, 12–13, 22–23; 1 Cor 15:45–49;
Luke 6:27–38

*Do to others as you would have them do to you.*

There's a popular saying going around: "Don't get mad; get even." Jesus says no to this and to a lot of other accepted wisdom. Today we get a large dose of idealism, expressed with soaring, unforgettable eloquence. But what are we to make of some of the things he says?

"Love your enemies."
"Turn the other cheek."
"Give to everyone who asks of you."
"Stop judging and you will not be judged."

There are three *wrong* ways to take these sayings:

1. Look on them as rules to be strictly obeyed.
2. Dismiss them as impractical and unrealistic.
3. Water them down.

Jesus is not indulging in empty rhetoric; he means to be taken seriously. But he is not making rigid rules of conduct. He is offering us ideals and challenging us to live them.

*Love your enemies.* Loving is not the same as liking. It's impossible to like everybody, and we don't have to. *Liking* is about how we *feel,* and we don't have control over our feelings. But we do have control over how we *act,* and love is proved not by words but by deeds. Do no evil, even to those who deserve it.

*Turn the other cheek.* This is not to be taken literally. It describes an ideal, an attitude. Break the circle of violence. Stop looking for revenge. Know when to let go of your anger. This ideal offers the only hope for peace in places like Israel, Northern Ireland, Rwanda, the Middle East, and the world's trouble spots. There was once a religious sister who was raising money for the poor in an anti-Catholic part of this country. After her talk, a mild-looking old man walked up to her. Expecting a donation, she held out her hand. He spat in it. She coolly wiped off her hand, held it out again, and said to him, "Okay, that's for me. Now, what do you have for Christ's poor?"

This refusal to get revenge, to get even, shows up not only in conflicts but also in an attitude of generosity. *Give to everyone who asks of you.* Once again, we must not take this literally. Jesus asks us to have an attitude of generosity that at least sometimes translates into action, even when expecting nothing in return.

*Stop judging.* Of course we have to judge what people *do,* when what they do is wrong and hurtful to others. But while you pass judgment on actions, resist the temptation to pass judgment on people. Only God can do that. Hate the sin, love the sinner.

In a word, "Be merciful, just as your Father is merciful." Try to be as generous and broadminded and forgiving as God! You'll never match God, or even come close. But just the effort will make you and the world around you better—less violent, less vengeful, more tolerant, more forgiving, more generous. To do so, you will have to struggle against some very basic human instincts—the desire to get even, the fear of being taken advantage of, the arrogant assumption that we can ever fully know what goes on in the mind and heart of another human being. It's hard, but not impossible. God's grace is there to help us. If it weren't, Jesus would never have asked us to try.

*Is there one of these ideals that you have fallen short of but feel called to pursue? What do you need to do?*

Sir 27:4–7; 1 Cor 15:54–58; Luke 6:39–45

*Remove the wooden beam from your eye first.*

Psychologists tell us that often those things we most dislike in others tend to be our own undesirable characteristics. Jesus says that we should look within ourselves before we blame others. We should be more concerned about the goodness of our own hearts than about the misdeeds of others.

In last Sunday's reading, Jesus told us not to judge. We may judge people's actions, but not the people themselves. We cannot read hearts and minds, not completely. And yet, people do things that make us rightly indignant. We can't ignore what's right in front of our eyes. Righteous anger is all right; Jesus himself showed it from time to time. But we must not let our anger eat us up. One thing that can help is to admit our own failings; this can help us to be more tolerant. Sometimes people can be so deluded, so unaware of their own shortcomings, that when they criticize others, Jesus calls them hypocrites. That's strong language! Most of us are not that blind, just a bit nearsighted.

We know we're not perfect, but, without putting it into words, we tend to think: "My faults are nice faults." Other people are stubborn; I'm consistent. They're lazy, but I'm easygoing. Some of them are irresponsible, whereas I'm devil-may-care. Other people are superficial; I'm mellow. Others nag; I'm just concerned. They're cowardly; I'm prudent. Some people are tactless; I just tell it like it is.

What makes us so tolerant toward ourselves? We know we're weak; we know we screw up from time to time. But we know that inside us there's a basically good person trying to get out. Well, Jesus says maybe that's true of the other person. Dealing with our anger at others is often difficult because it involves not just our thoughts but also our emotions, which are not subject to our control. There are some wounds that only time can heal. Just getting older can be a help. It's not a guarantee; some old people just get more and more bitter. But there are some happy stories of reconciliation. We older folks know this from experience. We look back on some of the battles we waged in our younger years and we wonder why they seemed so important at the time. It's not just a matter of mellowing; it's a gaining of perspective, a ripening into wisdom. If we could relive those stormy times, we'd try to be more tolerant and understanding.

Well, all this is easy to talk about but not so easy to do. Right now I'm trying to deal with my righteous anger at someone, and not doing too well. I can't help feeling the way I do, but I'm responsible for the way I act. So are we all. If any of you have been down this road, let's take Jesus' words to heart. Let's pray for one another. During Mass, let's ask the Lord to heal our nearsightedness, to help us see ourselves as he does. Then we will be healthy trees that bring forth good fruit. Out of the fullness of our hearts, our mouths will speak only what is good.

*Are there any ways in which you tend to be too easy on yourself or too hard on others?*

## Ninth Sunday of the Year

1 Kgs 8:41–43; Gal 1:1–2, 6–10; Luke 7:1–10

*I tell you, not even in Israel have I found such faith.*

In today's gospel we meet an extraordinary man who rose above his environment. We don't know his name, but we know a great deal about him. He has a lot to tell us not only about his own time but also about ours; and what we learn about him encourages us to ask questions about ourselves.

The centurion was a high-ranking officer in the Roman army. Centurions had to be real leaders—disciplined, courageous, and resourceful—and they formed the backbone of the most powerful armed force in the ancient world. This man served in a force that was occupying a foreign land, and the men who served with and under him knew what it was to hate and to be hated. Most of the soldiers despised the Jews and pushed them around, and the Jews responded with understandable resentment and hatred. But this centurion was different. He was on respectful, friendly terms with the Jewish people. He had made contributions to the building of their synagogue, and the leading men were so grateful that they were glad to speak for him and ask Jesus for help.

This was not the only way that he stood out from the crowd. His attitude toward his sick slave was extraordinary for his times. Slaves were not considered persons. They were things, to be used and abused and thrown aside. For a high-ranking person to be so concerned about the well-being of a slave was unusual, but this centurion is no ordinary man. When he enlists the aid of the elders, he shows tact and sensitivity toward their religious customs. He knows that Jews are not supposed to receive Gentiles in their homes, and that they are even more strictly forbidden to enter the homes of Gentiles. So he sends a message asking Jesus to heal his slave without coming to his house; in this way he would avoid giving offense. Not only was the centurion a tolerant, tactful, sensitive person; he was also a man of great faith. He recognized in Jesus a man who, like him, wielded authority and power. So he tells Jesus, "You don't have to come; just say the word, and my servant will be healed." Even Jesus himself was amazed at the man's faith; he said it was hard to find even among his own people.

There are times when we all have to rise above our environment. Though we live in a great country among many of the finest people in the world, there are aspects of our culture that are unhealthy. Consumerism, sexual irresponsibility, racial and ethnic prejudice, excessive individualism, lack of respect for life, and a casual, dismissive attitude toward religion are all around us. To rise above them, we need some of the centurion's qualities: independence of mind, strength of character, and strong religious faith. Later in this Mass we will pay tribute to him when we use his very words. Just before receiving communion, we will say, "Lord, I am not worthy to receive you; but only say the word, and I shall be healed."

*In what concrete situations in my life does this gospel challenge me to rise above my environment? How can I do it?*

## Tenth Sunday of the Year

1 Kgs 17:17–24; Gal 1:11–19; Luke 7:11–17

*Young man, I tell you, arise!*

When Jesus saw the funeral procession, did it make him think of his mother? The death of a young man is always tragic, but it was doubly so in this case, because he was the only child of a widowed mother. In that society, she would be left alone and destitute. Later on, when Jesus was dying on the cross, he asked John to look after his own mother.

Luke tells us that Jesus was "moved with pity." He uses a word that the gospels often use to describe Jesus' reaction to human suffering. We do well to watch Jesus closely, for his behavior always tells us something about God. The apostle

Philip once asked Jesus what God the Father was like. Jesus replied by assuring Philip, "Whoever has seen me has seen the Father" (John 14:9). The Word was made flesh in order to tell us things about God that we would never have imagined. When we think about God, the words *almighty, majestic, all-knowing, infinite* come to mind. We know him as Creator, Lord, and Judge. But "deeply moved"? Now we know that we are not the only ones who feel crushed by an untimely death and weep at a funeral. Jesus shows us that God is not above it all; he is with us, and shares the pain.

So Jesus calls the young man back to life and returns him to his mother. Raising the young man was a miracle, but it was also a sign. Now we know that Jesus not only shares our lot; he is also the lord of life and death, and his power is to heal and to save. We know that he calls us to the fullness of life, to a life stronger than death.

*How does watching Jesus help me relate to a God who sometimes seems distant and unresponsive to my pain and need?*

## Eleventh Sunday of the Year

2 Sam 12:7–10, 13; Gal 2:16, 19–21; Luke 7:36—8:3

*Her many sins have been forgiven, because
she has shown great love.*

As we grow older, certain memories stay with us instead of fading with time. Some of these memories endure because they are gratifying, some because they are unpleasant and still give us pain, and some leave us with mixed feelings. During his public life, Jesus had many vivid experiences that must have stayed with him long after they were over. What about this one? It was one of many incidents that we meet in the gospels in which Jesus takes on his enemies and vanquishes them. Their attacks were usually unprovoked, calculating, and vicious; time and again, he showed them up and made them look bad. There was a part of Jesus that must have felt satisfaction at having told off this Pharisee. He was just as human as we are, and you know how good it feels to tell off someone who's looking for trouble and deserves what he gets.

The Pharisee certainly deserved to be shown up. He had broken some of his society's basic rules of hospitality. When a guest was invited to dinner, the host was supposed to place his hand on his shoulder and give him a kiss of peace. The visitor's feet would be very dusty, since the roads were dirt tracks and people wore sandals instead of shoes. So cool water was poured over them to make them clean and comfortable. The host was expected to put a pinch of incense or perfume on his guest's head. All these marks of respect were especially appropriate when the guest was a distinguished rabbi like Jesus, and none of them was observed. It makes you wonder why he invited Jesus in the first place. He doesn't seem to be attacking him or laying a trap for him; the atmosphere is not that hostile. But his whole manner is patronizing. He thinks this well-known young Galilean rabbi rates an invitation, but he spoils the occasion by not even trying to conceal his contempt.

Maybe Jesus might have given him a free pass and written him off as a boor and the dinner as a lost evening. But then the sinful woman comes in. She shows Jesus the marks of respect that had been omitted, and she expresses her misery and repentance for the life she has been reduced to. The Pharisee is not just embarrassed at this remarkable scene, he is disgusted. He looks down at the woman from his lofty perch of self-righteousness and sees nothing but a human failure who deserves an extra dose of his large store of contempt. And that's when Jesus lets him have it. He won't stand on his own dignity, but he will not stand by while a hypocrite sits in judgment on a sinner doing penance.

Before this memorable scene plays out, Jesus makes an extraordinary statement. "Her many sins have been forgiven because she has shown great love." Is he saying that it's all right to do wrong as long as you do some good? No, Jesus never made light of sin. But he gives us an insight into the way his Father looks at us. God doesn't close his eyes to our failings, but he is much more interested in the good parts of our lives and sets greater store by them. He's a lot like us. We all have friends and family who are dear to us. We know their annoying little quirks that bother us, and their faults that disturb and disappoint us, but we love and respect them for all the good that we see in them. That's how God feels about us.

*When you consider how you stand in the sight of God, imagine him adding up your good deeds as well as your sins. Sneak a peek at the list.*

## Twelfth Sunday of the Year

### Zech 12:10–11, 13:1; Gal 3:26–29; Luke 9:18–24

*Whoever wishes to save his life will lose it.*

At the end of World War II, the Allies found written and photographed records that had been kept by the Nazis. A set of pictures taken by a German staff photographer records an incident that took place in July 1941 outside a village in Yugoslavia. The Germans had conquered and occupied that area. Some of the villagers had committed sabotage, and now the Germans were taking reprisal. They lined up a group of peasants before a firing squad. The soldiers took aim—all except one. Private Joseph Schultz refused to participate. Nothing that his commanding officer said could change his mind. So he was lined up with the hostages and shot to death by his comrades. When you look at those photos, the tragedy tears at you. What a waste! A young man loses his life—for what? The hostages died anyway, and he made just one more. What did he accomplish?

The answer is given by Jesus Christ. He says that if you try too hard to save your life, you will lose it. Joseph Schultz knew what he meant. This young man, with his whole life before him, knew that if he participated in murder he would save his life on one level; but on a deeper level, he would lose it. Indeed, he would lose his very self. So he chose to be a martyr of conscience. On that day, in a dark tableau of death and destruction, he was a shining light, a true hero, an example of everything that is best in a human life.

And what of the other soldiers, his comrades, the ones who killed rather than be killed? If some of them are still living, they are old men now. You wonder how they live with what they did. Can you blame them for holding on to life? And yet the words of Jesus, and the action of Joseph Schultz, do not go away. Those men saved their lives, but something in them died.

Most people do not have to make such terrible life-or-death choices. But in order to follow Christ, somewhere along the line, choices must be made. To retain our integrity, we may have to lose money. To be true to ourselves, we may be forced to lose a friend. To be able to look in the mirror, we may have to sacrifice the esteem of people whose opinion matters to us. The path that Jesus chose led inevitably to the cross, and following him does the same for us. But the cross is not the end of the story—not for him, not for Joseph Schultz, and not for us. On the other side of death is the fullness of life.

*Is God asking me to take a stand?*

1 Kgs 19:16b, 19–21; Gal 5:1, 13–18; Luke 9:51–62

*I will follow you wherever you go.*

Today's readings are all about *following*. The prophet Elijah calls Elisha, who leaves everything to follow him. Paul tells the Galatians to renounce their selfish desires and to follow the Spirit, who will make them truly free. In the gospel account, three men volunteer to follow Jesus; he says it's going to cost them. He has no fixed address; they must come on board immediately, leaving their families and everything else behind. This makes following Christ sound very demanding; is it really as hard as Jesus makes it out to be?

Most of us don't think of our religion as making dramatic demands of us. We know that religion *can* be conventional, safe, devoid of idealism—a way simply to fit in. So are we luke-warm Christians? How can we tell?

The early Christians knew they had to be different from their fellow citizens in the decadent Roman Empire. What about us today? Sometimes being a good Christian means just to live up to what is best in the American way of life: honesty, generosity, fair play, justice, compassion. But sometimes we have to be different; Christianity *is* countercultural. The most obvious contrast is in the area of sexual morality—what we call "family values." We insist that children have a right to be brought into this world by parents pledged to care for them and for each other. We say that the search for happiness and meaning in our lives has to go beyond making money and conspicuous consumption. We stand for the sacredness of life against a pervasive culture of death; we renounce abortion, euthanasia, and assisted suicide.

These are our values. Sometimes when we stand up for them we provoke resentment. Today's anti-Catholicism is not religious; it's moral. People don't like to be told that what they're doing is wrong. To many of our fellow citizens, we come across as puritanical and oppressive. But the things we oppose do real damage, and the command to love our neighbor demands that we speak out, sometimes in words, always by what we are. Today children come into the world in all kinds of ambiguous circumstances. The damage is all around us, obvious to all but those who do not want to see.

Living up to standards of Christian morality isn't always difficult, but from time to time it may call for sacrifice, unselfishness, and self-restraint. These are bad words among the people who write many of our songs, our television scripts, and movie screenplays. They want us to feel out of it, joyless, and old-fashioned. But there are a lot of people out there, not of our faith, who agree with us—many more than the mass media would have you believe.

Talking this way doesn't mean that we consider ourselves superior or look down on others. We have our faults and our weaknesses like everyone else; we are all sinners. But to be a Christian is to aim high. We try to respond to Jesus' invitation to follow him whether the way is easy or hard. His way is the only one fully worthy of a human being. It makes life better for everyone. And it brings out the best in all of us.

*In order to follow Christ faithfully, have I sometimes been called to leave something or someone behind?*

Isa 66:10–14c; Gal 6:14–18; Luke 10:1–12, 17–20

*Ask the master of the harvest to send out
laborers for his harvest.*

Today's gospel reading tells of Jesus sending out his disciples to preach his message and carry on his work. This is a good time to talk about priests.

It's not a happy subject. Priests are getting older and fewer, and many of us have betrayed their people and damaged the church in the eyes of the world. But we all have a stake in the priesthood, so the church has been taking a hard look at the past in order to find out what went wrong and why, and how to keep it from happening again. For a few minutes, let's talk not about the past but about the future. What does Jesus say about priests? What does he expect of them, and what should we?

First of all, priests have to be idealists. They must have an itch to share, a fire in the belly that drives them to give of themselves. If they are going to be more than pious functionaries, they must be men on a mission. They must resist the siren call of careerism that equates success with climbing the ladder of clerical promotion. That's a big order. But we all know many men who fit this description; they live lives of generous, effective ministry, and they deserve the gratitude and admiration of those they serve.

Jesus tells them to travel light. He says they should accept food and lodging from the people, for "the laborer is worth his wage." Priests deserve a decent living, but this is no way to get rich. When I was teaching school, I asked my students why there are fewer and fewer priests. This is what one of them wrote: "When boys grow up, they see that the people who seem to enjoy life are the well-off people. The working students do want to go to a good college; they don't want to waste their work on a life of little means as a priest. They want to be worth something."

*To be worth something.* What a revealing line! It tells us that celibacy is not the only problem. A shallow culture, a whole way of life has to be rejected before a man can respond to the call of Christ and live up to it. He has to find his satisfaction in something other than earning, buying, owning, and consuming. Why are we surprised that fewer and fewer Americans are signing up?

And yet Jesus says, "The harvest is abundant but the laborers are few; so ask the master of the harvest to send out laborers for his harvest." The master of the harvest is the Holy Spirit. So what's the problem? Is the Spirit calling young men to the priesthood, and they're not listening? Or is the Spirit calling others, and we're not listening? The church has to face the questions that many are asking: Should we have married priests? Are women also called? These are serious questions, not to be lightly answered or easily dismissed. Let's pray that we and our leaders listen to the Spirit and send laborers for the harvest. There's a lot waiting to be done.

*Think of a priest you know and admire. How does he live values that transcend those of our consumer culture?*

## Fifteenth Sunday of the Year

Deut 30:10–14; Col 1:15–20; Luke 10:25–37

*A Samaritan traveler who came upon him
was moved with compassion.*

When we hear or read, in the news of the day, that a person went out of his or her way to help someone in need, they are often called a "good Samaritan." This parable has become part of our language.

At first hearing, the meaning of the parable seems clear: if you see someone in need or in danger, you should reach out to that person, even at cost to yourself. If that's all it means, then we don't need this homily; the story speaks for itself. But there's more to it. If that was all Jesus wanted to tell his hearers, he shouldn't have made the hero a Samaritan. We say good Samaritan, but as far as many of the Jewish people of that time were concerned, the only good Samaritan was a dead Samaritan! For centuries there had been deep-seated hatred between the two peoples. Today, for "Samaritan" read "Palestinian," and you get the idea.

The lawyer asks Jesus, "*Who* is my neighbor?" [emphasis added]. At first sight Jesus instead seems to tell him *what* it means to be a neighbor—to reach out and help. But in a subtle way he tells him *who* the neighbor is by making him not a fellow Jew but a foreigner, an outsider, a member of a despised ethnic group. In the battered, bleeding man by the side of the road, the Samaritan sees not a Jew but a fellow human being who desperately needs his help. And he does what we all like to think we would have done in those circumstances.

This story must have bothered those who first heard it; it was threatening to them. What about us? The name Samaritan has no negative connotation today. But think of other names of other races, other nationalities, other religions, other ethnic groups. Do any of them arouse negative feelings in you? If you feel no hostility at all to any of them, you are most unusual. It means you have grasped one of the central features of Jesus' message: that in the sight of God, differences of race, nationality, and sex have no importance compared to our common humanity. Christianity is a universal religion. It teaches that all men and women are sons and daughters of God, members of one great big family, all equally deserving of our respect and concern. There is no place for prejudice, disrespect, or discrimination. It is obvious that this is one of Christianity's greatest failures. Down through the centuries and in our own day, Catholics and other Christians have a sad history of tribalism, a spirit of "us" against "them" that makes us fall short of the ideal.

It's not surprising that we stumble. In asking us to go beyond tribalism, Jesus asks us to overcome a basic human instinct. It's like when he asks us to overcome such feelings as the desire for revenge. Don't be fooled by the common saying that "all religions say the same thing." They don't. Christianity is a very idealistic, demanding faith. Without God's grace, we couldn't even come close to living up to it. But the good Samaritan did. And what Jesus said to the lawyer, he says to you and me, "Go and do likewise."

*How do I deal with the negative feelings I experience toward people who are different?*

## Sixteenth Sunday of the Year

Gen 18:1–10a; Col 1:24–28; Luke 10:38–42

*Mary has chosen the better part.*

Mary spends time listening to Jesus because he opens up a whole world to her. Paul calls it "the mystery hidden from ages and from generations past…but now…manifested to his holy ones."

Many people are totally closed off from this mystery; it is a world they find totally unreal. A friend of mine once told me about a challenging conversation he had with a lawyer. The man told him, "You clergymen try to convince people that they are more than animals. You try to make them believe that there is some transcendent purpose to life, that there is some kind of cosmic meaning that they can be part of. The way I see it, if we have any purpose on this earth, it is just to keep things going. We can stir the pot while we are here and try to keep things interesting. Beyond that, everything runs down: your marriage runs down, your body runs down, your faith runs down. We can only try to make it interesting."

The lawyer, of course, is an atheist. He says, in effect, that what you see is what you get, and nothing more. We disagree. By our very presence here at this Eucharist, we are saying that he is wrong. There is a whole dimension of reality that escapes him. It can be seen only with the eyes of faith. We have been let in on a secret: that we are not alone in an uncaring universe that's going nowhere. We are loved and cared for by a God who, through Jesus Christ, has shared our lot. By his cross and resurrection he has won for us a life stronger than death. Yes, things run down, but that's not the last word. God has a plan for us, and a destiny. He invites us on a journey to a fuller life.

To outsiders, we are just a group of people engaged in ritual behavior here at Mass. But much more is going on. We are in touch with the world of the spirit. We are engaged in a conversation with the living God who is not a million miles away but right here among us, as close as Jesus was to Mary. We are making present the redemptive death and resurrection of God's own son. We are eating the bread of life—Jesus himself—as food for the journey.

We have much reason to be grateful, to rejoice, to hope. Do we have anything to *do*? Yes. We can share the secret with those who have not heard the good news or, like the lawyer, find it hard to believe. How can we do that?

- just by being here, in church, we are making a statement;

- by trying to live lives marked by justice and compassion and care;
- by refusing to settle for a life of conspicuous consumption;
- by valuing people more than things.

These are signs that this liturgy is no mere exercise in empty religious formalism, but that we are truly in touch with the divine.

The lawyer says, "In the end, everything runs down."

St. Paul says, "What eye has not seen, and ear has not heard, / and what has not entered the human heart, / what God has prepared for those who love him" (1 Cor 2:9). And they're happening right here, right now.

*How much of Jesus' friend Mary, and how much of the lawyer, do I find in myself?*

## Seventeenth Sunday of the Year

**Gen 18:20–32; Col 2:12–14; Luke 11:1–13**

*Ask and you will receive.*

Today's readings are about the power of prayer. In the first reading, Abraham pleads with God to spare the people of Sodom and Gomorrah. In the gospel passage, Jesus urges us to ask his Father for what we need and assures us that our prayers will be answered. For some of us, that's enough to keep us praying. But sometimes we wonder: Doesn't God know what we need? Does God need reminding? And how about the times when we don't get what we asked for?

Good questions! There are no easy answers because we can't even begin to understand God, who always eludes our comprehension. And Jesus doesn't try to explain either. But he is very clear about what we are supposed to *do*. He tells us to ask, to search, to keep knocking on the door, and he assures us that the door will be opened.

In the gospels, Jesus is usually portrayed as a person of great patience. But sometimes he shows impatience, even resentment, at people who do not trust his Father to take care of them. This is one of those passages. Listen to him: "What father among you would hand his son a snake when he asks for a fish? Or hand him a scorpion when he asks for an egg? If you then, who are wicked, know how to give good gifts to your children, how much more will the Father in heaven give the Holy Spirit to those who ask him?" Do you blame him for being impatient? After all God has done for us, how could we not trust? It's as if we asked God: "What have you done for us lately?"

But what about the times when we didn't get what we asked for? Well, those of you who have children know that sometimes they ask for things that are not good for them. Sometimes you just can't give them all you want to. It's the same with God. But Jesus assures us that no prayer goes unanswered; every prayer is answered in some way.

He says, "Ask and you will receive."

What will you receive? He doesn't say.

"Seek and you will find."

Find what? Maybe not what we're looking for. Maybe something better.

"Knock and the door will be opened."

What is behind the door, he doesn't say. But one thing is sure. Behind that door is a loving, caring God who is faithful, who will never abandon us. Don't ever doubt that, not for a minute.

*How do I deal with feelings of disappointment or discouragement when my prayers seem to go unanswered?*

## Eighteenth Sunday of the Year

### Eccl 1:2; 2:21–23; Col 3:1–5, 9–11; Luke 12:13–21

*One's life does not consist of possessions.*

The farmer in this story had the kind of problem that any farmer would love to have. His harvest was so good that his barns needed to be enlarged. Wonderful! Who can blame him for his reaction? "Relax! Eat heartily, drink well, enjoy yourself." Of course. And yet....

The author of our first reading feels sorry for him. Why? Because, in the words of a great old-time play and movie, *You Can't Take It with You.* When he dies, the result of all his work and planning and anxiety will be gone, passed on to someone else. Well, okay, we knew that. It's not a very profound observation.

But in the gospel reading, Jesus is much harder on him. He has God call him a fool. Why? Why not feel good about the success of his business? What's wrong with eating and drinking and enjoying yourself? Is God a wet blanket? No, God criticizes him not for anything he *does* but for what he *doesn't* do. Listen to him. It's all about *me, me, me. I* got it made. *I* can relax. *I* can eat in the best restaurants. *I* can enjoy myself. We hear nothing about anyone else in his life. Nothing about sharing his good fortune with others. Nothing about giving to the poor. He sounds utterly self-absorbed, locked up in a very small world in which no one but him seems to matter. You get the feeling that when he dies, no one will miss him, either.

Jesus' comment goes right to the heart of this sad story: "Thus will it be for the one who stores up treasure for himself but is not rich in what matters to God."

Well, we've all had similar thoughts about rich people who are too greedy to care about those who are less fortunate. It's hard for us to apply this parable to ourselves. We don't think of ourselves as rich. But money is not the only form of wealth. Each of us has some talent, some skill, some personal quality that could enrich the lives of those around us. It's not just a matter of sharing our money, but of sharing ourselves. We all must strive not to get too wrapped up in ourselves; that's a lifetime job. If we manage to break out of the small world of self and reach out to others, Jesus assures us that we will be rich in the sight of God. And that's something you *can* take with you.

*Do I have gifts—material or spiritual—that God is waiting for me to share?*

## Nineteenth Sunday of the Year

**Wis 18:6–9; Heb 11:1–2, 8–19; Luke 12:32–48**

*Where your treasure is, there also will your heart be.*

There was a movie, many years ago, about an inventor who almost causes a huge financial crisis. He invents a fabric that doesn't wear out. It seems like a great discovery until people realize that owning an indestructible suit means you'll never have to buy another one. What will happen to all the people who make their living in the garment industry? A big part of the business world depends for its very survival on the assurance that things will wear out and have to be replaced. (Don't ask me how the movie turned out. I forget.)

Jesus tells us to get purses that do not wear out, that are moth-proof and guaranteed never to be stolen. He calls it "an inexhaustible treasure in heaven…" (Luke 12:33). What is he talking about? Well, everything we own eventually wears out: clothes, shoes, furniture, cars, even our homes. Are there any things in our lives that last—things that in the sight of God never lose their value and endure forever? How about these: Being faithful in love. Raising a child. Giving to someone in need. Forgiving an enemy. Visiting the sick. Taking time to pray and worship. Working and sacrificing for a good cause. Telling the truth, even at cost. We may take for granted these good things we do, but God does not. They are assets in our account that show up in time and in eternity.

At the end of our lives, we will render an account to God. Jesus urges us to be ready for that day, which may come when we least expect it. We don't have to know the day or the hour, for we will die pretty much the way we lived. So we just keep trying, here and now, to do the good and avoid the bad, and the rest will take care of itself. How would we like God to find us at the end of life? At peace with ourselves, at peace with our neighbor, and at peace with God. It would be nice if we could leave this life knowing that our work is completed. Jesus himself, in John's Gospel, prays to his Father, "I glorified you on earth by accomplishing the work you gave me to do" (John 17:4). Maybe there are things waiting to be done—asking for pardon, renewing a friendship, patching up a quarrel, paying a debt, checking up on someone who is alone. We should do them before time runs out on us.

In a world where most things pass away, these are the things that last. They are the never-failing treasure with the Lord. Jesus says, "Where your treasure is, there also will your heart be." And St. Paul writes, "If then you were raised with Christ, seek what is above" (Col 3:1).

*Think of some good things in my life that are not likely to wear out, and some that are waiting to be done.*

## Twentieth Sunday of the Year

Jer 38:4–6, 8–10; Heb 12:1–4; Luke 12:49–53

*I have come to set the earth on fire.*

Later in this Mass, we will remember what Jesus told his disciples, "Peace I leave you, my peace I give to you," and we will then exchange a greeting of peace. But in today's gospel reading, Jesus tells us that he has come not to establish peace on the earth but rather for division. Can he have it both ways? What are we to make of this?

*Peace* means different things to different people and in different times. To some, peace means that everything is quiet, there are no disturbances; law and order prevail. These *may* be signs of real peace, but maybe not. Underneath the surface tranquility, there may be injustice, racism, sexism, ageism, economic exploitation, religious discrimination, and many other kinds of oppression. There may be laws passed to perpetuate these kinds of oppression, and people can get into trouble for protesting or acting against them. That's not real peace; that's violence disguised as respectability. The command to love our neighbor obliges us to protest against mistreatment and to struggle for justice. That can create division. It can even get people thrown into jail. When Martin Luther King, Jr. and others fought for racial justice, they were called "outside agitators." They followed the example of Jesus and tried to "set the earth on fire." Thank God, they succeeded!

Today our country is not at peace. Yes, we are threatened by terrorists, but they are not the only enemy. The terrorists do not divide us; we are united in opposing them. But peace is also threatened from within. We cannot say that as a nation we are truly at peace, as long as millions go without health insurance; as long as minorities are treated differently from others by law enforcement; as long as women are paid less than men for the same kind of work; as long as special interests are allowed to destroy our environment; as long as gentrified neighborhoods leave whole families out on the street; as long as prosecutors put innocent defendants on death row; as long as unborn children are deprived of their right to life.

When we Catholics and other Christians and other people of good will protest against these violations of human dignity, we are called divisive. Many of our fellow citizens aspire to a false kind of peace; to them we seem like the prophet Jeremiah, disturbers of their complacency. We sin against what seems to be a highly regarded virtue among Americans—not to cause anyone pain, or to feel another's pain. Since in this country they are not allowed to silence us, they treat us like outsiders or just ignore us. We shouldn't be surprised; prophets have always been treated that way.

What would Jesus say about how we live today? He would see much that is good, but also much that still needs to be done. What kinds of fires would he like to start around here?

*Are there any fires that need lighting that I might help ignite?*

## Twenty-First Sunday of the Year

**Isa 66:18–21; Heb 12:5–7, 11–13; Luke 13:22–30**

*Strive to enter through the narrow gate.*

In today's gospel someone asks Jesus the question that we have all wondered about: Will few, or many, be saved? Jesus doesn't answer directly. He says, try to squeeze through a narrow door. He doesn't say how many will make it, but he says clearly that some will not. In the first reading from Isaiah, God makes it clear that he wants everyone to be saved, but he will not force salvation on anyone. If some people fail to make it through the door, it is *their* choice, not God's.

Jesus says that on the day of reckoning there are going to be some surprises. People we never expected to meet in heaven will be there. Some who thought they had reserved seats are going to be turned away at the gate. Some who expected luxury boxes are in for a shock. They tell the story of a rich woman who was used to every luxury and to respect. She died and was admitted to heaven and was greeted by an angel who showed her around. They passed many impressively beautiful mansions; each time she thought the next one was hers. But they kept going, into a rundown neighborhood, and finally came to a hut. "This is yours," the angel said. "Oh," she said, "I can't live in that!" The angel replied, "I'm sorry we couldn't do better for you, but this is all we could put together with the materials you sent up."

Jesus warns his questioner, a member of the chosen people, that there are no guarantees. The same goes for us Christians who "ate and drank in [his] company" and in whose streets he taught. Sometimes it's going to be a struggle. In today's second reading, the writer of the letter to the Hebrews reminds us that God, like a loving parent, disciplines those he loves. Elsewhere in the Bible, Jesus is called a bridegroom, and discipleship is like a marriage. You know that you have to work at a marriage to keep it going. Stop working at it, get complacent, settle for routine, and it can run down.

Don't get the wrong idea. Jesus is not saying these things in order to scare us and make us get in line. He's just reminding us that the love of God and neighbor is a serious business. It includes a lot more than just keeping rules and staying out of trouble. He's being honest with us, telling us that following him is not always going to be a bed of roses; that sometimes it's going to *cost;* that we shouldn't be surprised when we are called upon to suffer. It's a narrow door, and sometimes it's a tight squeeze. But he is with us, always by our side, assuring us of his grace when we need it. We can always count on him. He just doesn't want to be taken for granted.

*Besides "keeping the rules" and staying out of trouble, what kinds of materials am I providing for my heavenly dwelling?*

## *Twenty-Second Sunday of the Year*

**Sir 3:17–18, 20, 28–29; Heb 12:18–19, 22–24a; Luke 14:1, 7–14**

*Everyone who exalts himself will be humbled, but the one who humbles himself will be exalted.*

We all care about what other people think of us. We want to be respected and to be taken seriously. Our reputation is important to us. And that's the way it should be. On the other hand, we would all agree that what other people think is not the last word about us, that we shouldn't take ourselves *too* seriously, and that there are times when our integrity and self-respect are more important than our reputation among others.

Jesus has some interesting things to say about all this in today's gospel reading. In the culture of his time, seating positions at a banquet served as a barometer of people's social standing. Important people got the best seats, and ordinary folks took what was left. He notices how his fellow guests are jockeying for positions of honor, and he gives them a tip: "Hey, you want to play this game right? Don't grab a spot at the head table. You could get bumped by some celebrity, and then you'll look bad. The smart thing is to take a seat at the back. Then your host will move you up the line, and you'll *really* look good." His suggestion sounds at first like just a clever way to manipulate one's neighbors and climb the social ladder, but I think he may have been just teasing them for taking a trivial business so seriously.

Then he takes the occasion to make a truly important point that we can all take to heart. Do you know whom we should really be trying to impress? Do you know whose opinion of us counts most of all? God, that's who. God knows, better than anyone, how I rate as a human being. God knows my good points and my bad points, my strengths and my weaknesses. I can fool some of the people some of the time, but I can't fool God. And most of us would probably be surprised to find out where we stand in the sight of God, which means in reality. Some of the things we do that others find most impressive may be far down on God's list. Conversely, some things about us that make no impression down here could be making us celebrities in heaven. As Jesus says, "Everyone who exalts himself will be humbled, but the one who humbles himself will be exalted." On another occasion, he said the first would be last and the last would be first.

Then, just to make sure that we get the point, he gives an example. The next time you throw a party, instead of rounding up the usual suspects, ask some of the people who don't get invited anywhere, the ones who can't give you anything in return. Reach out to the poor, to the unattractive, even to the ungrateful. God loves it when we do stuff like that. And he assures us that we will be repaid at the biggest dinner of all, in the resurrection of the just.

*What are some ways in which people overrate me and some ways in which they underrate me? How will God correct my report card?*

Wis 9:13–18b; Phlm 9–10, 12–17; Luke 14:25–33

*Whoever does not carry his own cross and come after me cannot be my disciple.*

Jesus says that anyone who wants to follow him must be ready to turn his back on family, on possessions, and even on his own life. Let's be honest; Even people who go to church, like ourselves, don't usually think of our religion as calling for these kinds of sacrifice. Oh, we know that martyrs give up their lives for Christ, but let's face it, we don't expect to be martyred. So what do these extraordinary demands of Jesus mean for ordinary people like us in our ordinary lives?

The first thing to notice is that Jesus makes this statement not just to the inner circle of his apostles, but to a great crowd. He means it not only for clergy and religious and missionaries, but for *everyone*. But how many think of religion this way? For many people, religion is just a nice thing to have. Church is a good place for christenings, weddings, and funerals. Our church also provides good schools. And everybody knows that religion is good for children. But discipleship, the following of Christ, is something more serious than that. It touches us at a deeper level. It affects our values, our priorities, and our loyalties, our whole way of looking at the world, at our work, at our lives and the lives of those closest to us.

There is only one other institution that makes these kinds of demands: our nation. In time of war, citizens expect to make sacrifices, even the ultimate sacrifice of dying for one's country. Christianity asks for no less. Jesus says that when it comes to following him, every other value or loyalty is subordinate. He compares it to being ready to carry a cross—and, thanks to Mel

Gibson, we know how painful *that* can be. Some of us know from experience what that can mean. Maybe we had to give up a habit, or a relationship, or a way of dealing with others, or a way of making money, or spending it. When he tells the parables of the man building a tower and the king going into battle, he is saying: "If you follow me, you'd better know what you're getting into. Get ready for the long haul."

We don't usually think of our faith this way. For the most part, our faith is a source of comfort and security, as it should be. But today we are reminded of an aspect of religion that is sometimes neglected: that it is a challenge, an inspiration, a summons to sacrifice, a call to greatness. If we let him, Jesus can bring out the best in us, more than we could ever do alone.

*Am I accepting the challenge of faith as well as its comfort?*

## Twenty-Fourth Sunday of the Year

Exod 32:7–11, 13–14; 1 Tim 1:12–17; Luke 15:1–32

*Rejoice with me because I have found my lost sheep.*

What is God like? How does God feel about us—about you and me? Jesus tells us through three stories: about a lost sheep, a lost coin, and a man whose son had gone wrong.

In the society of Jesus' time, many of the flocks of sheep were owned by the community; two or three shepherds were in charge. Sometimes the shepherds whose flocks were safe would return on time and tell the people that one of them was still out in the mountains searching for a lost sheep. The villagers would all be keeping watch, waiting for his return. When he appeared in the distance, with the sheep over his shoulders, the whole community would shout with joy. That's the picture that Jesus draws when he says there will be rejoicing in heaven over a sinner doing penance.

The coin that the woman lost was valuable. The floors of peasant dwellings were dirt and bulrushes; the light was poor. It was like looking for a needle in a haystack. The woman is so relieved when she finds it, that she's out in her backyard telling her friends the good news. What a picture of God! How literally down to earth!

In the third story, the man hasn't lost a sheep or a coin; he's lost his son. The kid couldn't wait for the old man to retire or die; he wanted his inheritance *now*. After blowing all the money, he comes home with his tail between his legs. The father sees him when he's still a long way off; he must have been looking for him. There are no recriminations. He doesn't even listen to the apology. All he says is, "You're back! Let's throw a party!"

These three stories are wonderful news for you and me—so wonderful, we're afraid to believe it. Our God is not a stern, unforgiving taskmaster who keeps track of all the bad and dumb things we do. He's a shepherd who works overtime to bring us back. He's a woman who's overjoyed at recovering something precious. He's a loving father who watches out for us even when we're a long way off. No matter how far we stray, God never stops reaching out to us and throws a party when we return.

So let's celebrate! Let's have a thanksgiving. Let's have a Eucharist.

*How do images of being lost and searching and finding figure in my relationship with God?*

Amos 8:4–7; 1 Tim 2:1–8; Luke 16:1–13

*No servant can serve two masters.*

In today's reading we are treated to a regular rogues' gallery
of thieves. The prophet Amos complains about people who
engage in price fixing and gouge the poor. In Jesus' parable, the
manager does a little price-fixing of his own to defraud the rich
man who is firing him. The tenants are dishonest, too, as they
go along with the manager's scheme. Even the rich man who's
being robbed gets a kick out of the whole operation; in prais-
ing the manager for his shrewdness, he indicates that he is
probably the most successful crook of them all.

All these characters are smart, but they're bad people. Amos
and Jesus both say that, in the end, God is going to get them.
Meanwhile, we can learn some valuable lessons about how to
handle money. Jesus points out that all these characters are clever
and resourceful not only in the way they fatten their bank
accounts, but also in how they network and make valuable
friends among other shady dealers. What honest people can learn
from them is not how to cut corners but how really to make the
best use of their money. In God's eyes, wealth carries with it a
responsibility. Not only how we *make* our money, but also how we
*spend* it says a lot about us. Some people squander their money
on pointless luxuries and waste it on trivial pursuits; they miss the
opportunity to do a lot of good. Others try to do the most good
they can for the people in their lives, for good causes, and for the
poor. Some of these are well-known philanthropists; most are just
ordinary people who do the best they can with what they have.

If you belong to this second group, Jesus has some good
news for you. He says, "You're making good use of the blessings

you have, spreading them around among those who need and deserve them the most. You share what you have with those who have less, and in this way you show that you're not trying to serve two masters. You own your money; it doesn't own you. When you have some extra cash on hand, you don't always think of what you can get for yourself; sometimes you look around to see where it could do the most good. Through your use of this world's goods, you are doing some really good networking. You are making friends not only here on earth but also in heaven, where you will get a good, lasting reception."

*How does Jesus make me think and feel about my spending habits?*

## Twenty-Sixth Sunday of the Year

Amos 6:1a, 4–7; 1 Tim 6:11–16; Luke 16:19–31

*Between us and you a great chasm is established.*

This is one of the most frightening passages in the Bible. The vivid description of hell as a state of unending torment is bad enough. What is even more disturbing is the realization of why the rich man is in hell. What did he do that was so terrible? The answer is nothing! He didn't do anything! And yet Jesus says he is punished for all eternity. If that scares you, well, maybe it should. That's why Jesus told the story—to scare the hell out of us.

Imagine if they took this story and made it into an episode for the TV series *Law and Order*. In the next-to-last scene, at the trial, the lawyer for the defense makes his closing statement. "Your honor, ladies and gentlemen of the jury, the prosecution has failed to make a case against my client. They haven't offered a shred of evidence against him. Not only did he do nothing to hurt the beggar; he didn't even notice him. He has not broken a single law. You have no choice but to declare him 'not guilty.'" And he's right, of course. The judge should have already dismissed the charges. That's the way the law works down here. But Jesus is talking about a "Higher Court."

Once when I was serving as a hospital chaplain, I was encouraging an elderly Catholic patient to return to the sacraments. He said he didn't need them. "How come?" I asked. He replied, "I love God, and I don't hurt anybody." Well, that's so far, so good. But was he in the clear? Maybe. Maybe not.

At the beginning of Mass, we sometimes pray, "I confess that I have sinned—in what I have done, and in what I have failed to do." Most days, when we look at ourselves, we can honestly say that we haven't done anything very wrong. But today we are asked to look at ourselves a little more closely. Is there anything important that I have *failed* to do? Is there anything missing in my life? Am I ignoring someone who needs me? Have I been putting off doing something that I know needs to be done? The rich man in the parable got so used to passing Lazarus at his door that he didn't even see him. Have I gotten used to things that ought to bother me?

Compared to the rich man in the parable, we all look pretty good. We don't lead lives of mindless luxury and self-indulgence. And we do feel compassion for the poor. We feel bad and maybe a bit guilty when we pass beggars on the street. We wish we could do more, and we feel helpless in the face of so much human suffering. But Jesus doesn't want to lay a guilt trip on us. He knows we can't solve all the world's problems. He just wants us to take a second look, to see if maybe there's something we can do, someone close by that we can help. As the Chinese say, "the longest journey starts with a single step."

*Looking back, do I regret missing opportunities to do good? Am I missing some now?*

## Twenty-Seventh Sunday of the Year

Hab 1:2, 3; 2:2–4; 2 Tim 1:6–8, 13–14; Luke 17:5–10

### *Increase our faith.*

Today's readings are all about the power of faith.

In the first reading, the prophet Habakkuk, writing around 600 BC, challenges God and calls him to account. The king of Babylon was plundering Israel. No human power was able to stop him. For centuries, the prophets had been proclaiming God's justice. So why was the Lord allowing injustice to triumph? God answers Habakkuk, "Justice will triumph, in God's good time. It will surely come, it will not be late." Meanwhile, we must live by faith.

In the second reading, Paul is writing from prison. He sees his execution coming, and this looks like a farewell letter to Timothy. He trusts in the Lord against all odds, and he tries to pass on that spirit to Timothy. He tells him to stand fast and not abandon the faith.

In the gospel reading, Jesus says this faith is the most powerful force in the world. He uses vivid, picturesque language to make his point, the way people of his time in the East used to do. He says if you had faith you could uproot a tree. Another time he talks about faith moving mountains. It's his way of saying that sometimes what seems impossible becomes possible if approached with faith.

When I was a boy, in the 1930s, I read in an old magazine, *Collier's,* that someday we would go to the moon. I said, "That's impossible." In 1954, when Roger Bannister became the first man to run the mile in under four minutes, someone predicted that one day they'd break three minutes, fifty seconds. I said, "That's impossible." Now the record is three minutes, forty-three seconds. In 1984, I turned off my TV when a game seemed surely over. So I missed one of the most famous plays in college football history, Doug Flutie's "impossible" touchdown pass that won the game.

If we approach a thing saying it can't be done, it won't be. If we approach it saying it must be done, the chances are it will. That's the power of faith. And these are just human accomplishments! Imagine what is possible when God is involved.

Is God involved? When we entered World War II, the heavyweight boxing champion Joe Louis joined the army. Reporters asked him what he thought would happen. Joe answered, with quiet confidence, "We'll win. God is on our side." And he was. And he still is.

*What are the things I do that I couldn't do without the gift of faith?*

## Twenty-Eighth Sunday of the Year

### 2 Kgs 5:14–17; 2 Tim 2:8–13; Luke 17:11–19

#### Where are the other nine?

For many years I was a teacher at an unusual private high school. It was partially endowed, charged no tuition, and was open to boys who won a place through a competitive examination. They were an impressive student body. I asked them if they were grateful to the family who had generously founded the school and made it possible for them to get an excellent education free of charge. Many of them said that, of course, they were grateful. But just as many said they were not. They said they had won their place through their own talent and effort, and didn't owe anything to anyone.

I think of those boys when I hear today's readings. The first group was like Naaman the Syrian and the Samaritan leper. They felt blessed by the kindness of strangers and wanted to give thanks as best they could. The second group was like the nine lepers who were cured, felt happy, and never thought of saying thank you. Why were they so ungrateful? The lepers didn't tell us, but the boys did, very clearly. They felt entitled. Whatever they got, they had coming to them.

We all know from experience that some people are better thankers than others. We know what it's like to go out of our way to do a favor for someone and then wait, in vain, to hear a thank you from them. Why are they like that? Maybe when they were children, their parents never taught them to say thank you. (I've seen that.) Maybe they're just self-absorbed. Maybe they simply feel that we, or life, owe them. Whatever the reason, the inability to feel gratitude or to express it is a real human failing.

There's a very interesting fact about Naaman the Syrian and the Samaritan leper. Both of them thank not only the prophet and Jesus; they thank God, as well. They remind us to be grateful not only to other people who have been kind to us but also to God, who is the most generous of all. There are so many good things in our lives that we tend to take for granted; maybe, without thinking about it, we feel entitled. Today we are reminded how much we owe to a wonderfully kind and generous God who has poured down on us so many blessings. How can we ever thank God enough? One way is through this celebration of the Eucharist. "Eucharist" is a Greek word meaning "thanksgiving." So let's get on with this Eucharist, our way of saying thank you to God.

*Is there some thanking I need to do, to people or to God?*

90

Exod 17:8–13; 2 Tim 3:14—4:2; Luke 18:1–8

*Will not God then secure the rights of his chosen ones?*

Today's readings give us two striking, unconventional images of God and of the power of prayer. In the first, Moses prays for his men in battle, and as long as he keeps his arms raised to God, they are victorious; if his arms droop from weariness, God will let them lose. In the second, Jesus compares God to a corrupt judge who's being worn out by a widow who keeps after him for justice, and finally gives in just to get her off his back.

This doesn't sound like the God that we know through human reason alone. Great thinkers have come to believe in the One they call the Supreme Being, "the God of the philosophers." He is almighty, all-knowing, unchanging. He governs the world with serene certainty. All seems determined; he has decreed what will happen. He knows our needs, and has decided what to do about them.

How different is the God of the Bible! Here we meet a passionate God, full of surprises. Keep those arms up, Moses, or you'll blow it! It's the same with Jesus. Over and over again, he urges us to ask our Father for what we need. But doesn't God know our needs? Why does he have to be asked? So don't argue! Just do it! Take him at his word when he says that to those who ask, it will be given.

Yeah, but we don't always get what we ask for. True, but sometimes we're better off. "Be careful what you ask for; you might get it." Whatever happens or doesn't happen, remember that we are loved and cared for. Even when God is silent, he is with us.

When Jesus needed words to tell us what God is like, he didn't call him Supreme Being. He called him Father. Those of us who are parents can't always give our children what we'd like to, even what they need. But we stand by them. God is like that. Jesus once said, "Which one of you would hand his son a stone when he asks for a loaf of bread, or a snake when he asks for a fish? If you then, who are wicked, know how to give good gifts to your children, how much more will your heavenly Father give good things to those who ask him" (Matt 7:9).

Maybe there are just some things that God can't take care of now. God has his reasons, and we can never know them all. But this we do know, and we have Jesus' word for it: God loves us, God watches over us, and God cares. In the end, it will be all right.

*How is my image of God reflected in the way I pray?*

## Thirtieth Sunday of the Year

Sir 35:12–14, 16–18; 2 Tim 4:6–8, 16–18; Luke 18:9–14

*Two people went up to the temple area to pray.*

At first sight, the lesson of today's gospel seems very simple. Jesus tells a parable urging us to be not proud but humble, especially when we pray. The proud Pharisee is the bad guy, the humble tax collector is the good guy. But there's more here than meets the eye.

When we hear the name "Pharisee" we think of Jesus' enemies whom he himself called hypocrites. Some of them were, but that wasn't the whole story. The Pharisees were not clergy; they were laymen who took God seriously and tried hard to live up to their religion. Listen to what this Pharisee thanks God for. He is not grasping or crooked. He doesn't cheat on his wife. He fasts twice a week. He makes generous donations to his synagogue. Hey, that's pretty good! He knows, and we know, that many people are stingy, that many are crooks, that they cheat on their spouses, live lives of self-indulgence, and get brain lock when the collection basket comes around. Like the Pharisee, we churchgoers try not to be like that, and we should be glad if we can honestly say that we do better. If we manage to be honest, faithful, and generous, we have good reason to thank God. So where did the Pharisee go wrong?

In his prayer, the Pharisee says he gives thanks to God. But does he really? Jesus describes him as one of "those who were convinced of their own righteousness" and who "exalt themselves." And we're not surprised. His whole manner indicates that he is self-satisfied and complacent. He doesn't see the good things in his life as coming from God's grace but from his own, unaided efforts. Maybe he doesn't know himself well enough to realize it, but he has come to the temple today not to thank God but to congratulate himself.

It gets worse. Not content with putting himself on a pedestal, he has to put down others as inferior. The tax collector looked like a good target for his contempt. The tax system imposed by the Romans was shot through with corruption; any Jew who worked for them was despised as a traitor. Jesus himself got a lot of bad press because he used to hang around such people. The Pharisee was right to condemn greed and dishonesty and infidelity, but he was wrong in passing judgment on another human being. He is arrogant enough to think that he knows all about the guy in the back pew; he doesn't see what God sees—a troubled man asking forgiveness for doing his job.

What about us? Like the Pharisee, we try to be good and live by God's standards. We know there's a lot of wickedness going on around us. We're right to condemn the evil that people do, but we must resist the temptation to think that we know what goes on in another human heart. We know a lot about sin, but not about sinners. Only God does.

## Thirty-First Sunday of the Year

**Wis 11:22—12:2; 2 Thess 1:11—2:2; Luke 19:1–10**

*Zacchaeus, come down.*

We have a saying about people who take risks. We say, "They've gone out on a limb." Zacchaeus went out on a limb, and it changed his life.

Why did Zacchaeus climb that tree? You expect children to do that, not adults. He had two reasons. First, it was the only way he could see Jesus over the heads of the crowd. He was short, and nobody made way for him because he was one of the most hated men in town. They despised him because he was a wealthy man who made a living working as a corrupt tax collector for the Roman occupiers. The second reason went much deeper. It wasn't just curiosity that sent him up that tree. Despite being wealthy, he was an unhappy, lonely man—an outcast. He had heard that this Jesus was friendly toward people like him, and he wanted to find out for himself.

He got even more than he hoped for. Jesus pays him a great honor by asking for an invitation to dinner at his home. Zacchaeus is so delighted that he announces that he's going to make restitution to the people he has cheated. This is the first day of the rest of his life; from now on, he's going to be a changed man. Jesus congratulates him for mending his ways; he says that salvation has come to his house this day. But when he says that he came to save a person who was lost, the word *lost* doesn't mean damned or doomed. It simply means *in the wrong place.* Zacchaeus had lost his way in life. He had made his money by cheating others, and found himself not only out of place among his neighbors, but also out of touch with his real, best self. Jesus helped him find his way back.

We all find ourselves sometimes in the wrong place. We get into habits, ways of acting or relating to others that we know are just not right. Jesus can help us find the courage to change, to find our way back to where we know we belong.

Well, this is a nice feel-good story with a happy ending. Or is it? Zacchaeus has to go home and tell his wife the good news; how is she going to take it? Having a guest for dinner on short notice is the least of her problems. After her husband gives back all that money, how are they going to live? Stay tuned for an exciting sequel. He's going to find out what we know from experience—that changing for the better isn't easy and sometimes calls for a lot of courage. We need all the help we can get. Fortunately, Jesus is always ready to give it to us. You don't have to climb a tree. Just ask.

*Recall a time when, like Zacchaeus, you were lost and then found.*

## Thirty-Second Sunday of the Year

2 Macc 7:1–2, 9–14; 2 Thess 2:16—3:5; Luke 20:27–38

*[God] is not God of the dead, but of the living.*

A young woman named Caroline once wrote an unusual letter to the *New York Times.* She was twenty-five, working at home as a free-lance copy editor, married to a successful young businessman, and the mother of two children. In it she says, "I am faced with the crisis of finding some meaning in life. No, my family is not enough. Yes, I want to make their lives as happy as possible. The question is, how do you find something to look forward to? Basically, what are goals of any kind in the face of death? How is it possible to be happy in the present, if there is no sense of accomplishing anything?"

This young woman was confronting her own mortality. People who knew her probably thought of her as someone who "had it all." But she was asking the most basic question about the meaning of life: what's the point, if it all ends with death?

There are different answers in every age. In Jesus' time, many of the Jewish people, including the Pharisees, believed in the resurrection of the dead, but the priests did not. Today many people believe in the immortality of the soul, but others have no such hope. Many look for something better in accounts of near-death experiences. And New Age spirituality encourages some to believe in a kind of reincarnation.

In today's readings we hear a message of unshakable hope in God's victory over sin and death. Seven brothers and their mother go to their deaths rather than break God's law. One of them cries out, "You are depriving us of this present life, but the King of the world will raise us up to live again forever." In the same spirit, Jesus reminds the priests that the One they worship is God not of the dead but of the living. He says that we become like angels and are no longer liable to death. We express our trust in God during the funeral Mass when we profess our belief that at death "life is changed, not taken away." This Eucharist is an expression of our belief in the good news that Christ is risen and has won for us a life stronger than death.

Yes, Caroline, there is a resurrection. Death does not have the last word. And those of us who believe can say, with the psalmist, "Lord, when your glory appears, my joy will be full. I in justice shall behold your face; on waking I shall be content in your presence."

*How do the readings help me to experience the consolation and hope that Caroline seeks and Paul prays for?*

Mal 3:19–20a; 2 Thess 3:7–12; Luke 21:5–19

*Not a hair on your head will be destroyed.*

Today's readings convey a troubling sense of impending doom of the end of the world as we know it. The prophet Malachi, writing five hundred years before Christ, sees the day of the Lord coming, when the proud and the evildoers will be destroyed by fire. Paul writes to the Thessalonians at a time when many Christians thought Christ's second coming was near; they were standing around idly, waiting for the end.

We find all this hard to relate to until the gospel reading gives us a jolt. Jesus is talking to people who are admiring the newly constructed temple, one of the great wonders of the world of his time. He says it will soon come crashing down, and then they will hear of wars and insurrections. Sound familiar? The Temple was their version of the Twin Towers. Their 9/11 was the siege and destruction of Jerusalem and the end of the Jewish nation. And as for wars and insurrections–well, we know all about them. This is a time when much of the world seems to have gone mad. We live in fear, waiting for the next disaster to strike. In a real sense, the world as we have known it *has* passed away, and we tremble to think of what may lie ahead.

In the face of these well-founded fears, we are told by God's spokespersons to face the future undismayed. Malachi says that on those who serve God, the sun of justice will rise. The psalmist sings that the Lord will come to rule the earth with justice. Paul tells the Thessalonians that the second coming is a long way off; meanwhile they are to live responsibly. Anyone who wants to eat has to work. Jesus assures us that God will never abandon us. He says that not a hair of our head will be harmed; that by patient endurance we will save our lives. This is not a message of mindless optimism. It does not guarantee that there will be no suffering or death. It is not based on boastful self-confidence, either. We are beyond that now; we know we are vulnerable. It is a message of hope based on confidence in God. Jesus says that there is no force destructive enough to justify despair. Meanwhile, we take Paul's advice. After taking all reasonable measures to preserve our security, we go about our daily lives doing our work and living up to our responsibilities. We can't help being afraid, but we refuse to give up hope. This is the only behavior worthy of those who believe in the God revealed by our Lord Jesus Christ.

*How can I face the fear we all share, with courage and determination?*

## Christ the King

**2 Sam 5:1–3; Col 1:12–20; Luke 23:35–43**

*This is the King of the Jews.*

At first sight, this looks like a strange gospel passage for the feast of Christ the King. In fact, it looks all wrong. The sign above his head calls him "the king of the Jews," but he looks like anything but a king. A king is supposed to be a powerful person; this one is utterly helpless, hanging from a cross. Kings have loyal subjects among their people; Jesus is abandoned by nearly all his followers. Kings usually project an intimidating presence; this one is being made fun of by his executioners and his enemies. Even unpopular kings command respect; this one is enduring a shameful execution in disgrace. Kings used to have the power of life and death over their subjects; this man's life is ebbing away by the hour. One of the men hanging on the cross next to him calls him a fraud. This thief insults Jesus and says, "If you are a real king, save yourself and us."

The one who sees beyond these contradictions is the man on the third cross, the one whom tradition calls the good thief. He admits his guilt, gives testimony to Jesus' innocence, and asks to be remembered when he comes into his kingdom. And he receives a promise of salvation that very day. A career criminal was the one who dimly perceived what we know clearly in the light of the resurrection: that Jesus was indeed the Messiah, who in the very act of dying was conquering death itself. This is the ultimate paradox: dying, he destroyed our death; rising, he restored our life. Paul, who met the risen Christ, calls him the image of the invisible God, the first-born of all creatures, who is before all else, who is the beginning, the first-born of the dead, so that primacy may be his in everything.

Yes indeed, Jesus Christ is a king. He reigns in the hearts of men and women throughout the world and down the ages. You cannot walk very far anywhere without seeing a cross on a building. In those buildings, people may be worshiping him, or teaching the young, or giving shelter to the homeless, or ministering to refugees and the poor, or healing the sick, or consoling the dying. What was once a sign of disgraceful death has for centuries been a marker pointing to so much that is good in people.

Kingship and royalty are hard for us to relate to today. Power is so often abused that we don't like to identify with it. But the power that Jesus wields from the cross is different. It seeks not to dominate but to reconcile, to heal, and to serve. The rule of Christ the King brings out the best in a world that needs all the help it can get.

*How does my accepting Christ as king involve accepting the cross?*

# Holy Days of Obligation

Rev 11:19a; 12:1–6a, 10ab; 1 Cor 15:20–27;
Luke 1:39–56

*The Almighty has done great things for me.*

Today's feast, the assumption of our Lady body and soul in heaven, celebrates the fullness of Mary's triumph over sin and death. It's a beautiful feast, but it seems, at first sight, to be a celebration of something wonderful that happened a long time ago to someone else and is far removed from our own lives. But that would miss the point.

Listen to Mary's stirring hymn, the Magnificat, in the gospel reading. She proclaims the historical revolution that began with the coming of the Savior—a change in the human condition:

[God] has shown the strength of his arm...
He has cast down the mighty from their thrones,
   and has lifted up the lowly.
He has filled the hungry with good things,
   and the rich he has sent away empty.

This revolution begins in the individual human heart, when men and women renounce selfishness and apathy and accept

God's invitation to generosity and justice. It reaches its fullness when it not only changes individuals but transforms social, political, and economic structures. In the past century it has dawned on the world that the poor and the lowly may topple oppressive powers. From Africa to Alabama, Martin Luther King, Jr. saw people rising and shaking off their chains. These were people who had discovered that they were God's children and that, because of that, they could not be enslaved.

Think of those other events in the past century and in our own lifetimes: when women got the vote; when racial segregation was outlawed; when the Berlin wall came down and the Soviet Union broke up; when South Africa abolished apartheid.

The mighty were cast down from their thrones and the lowly were lifted up.

Mary was a member of two oppressed minorities. She was a Jew living under Roman rule, and a woman in a patriarchal society. And her son was executed as a criminal, but he changed the world forever. His death and resurrection let loose powerful forces capable of transforming it into a kingdom of justice, love, and peace. It usually starts not with the rich or powerful but with the poor and lowly, like Rosa Parks. The struggle still goes on; there's always more to be done. Sometimes it looks hopeless, but then we remember Mary's triumph. She tells us, today, that the God who is mighty and has done great things for her can do great things for us, too, because his mercy is from age to age on those who fear him. And so, with Mary, we proclaim today the greatness of the Lord, and our spirits rejoice in God our savior.

*When I look around, where do I see the poor and the lowly changing things for the better?*

Rev 7:2–4, 9–14; 1 John 3:1–3; Matt 5:1–12a

*Rejoice and be glad, for your reward
will be great in heaven.*

A soldier was once seriously wounded in battle in a sixteenth-century brushfire war between French and Spanish forces. He spent months convalescing in his parents' home and asked for something to read. All they had were some pious books—a life of Christ and biographies of some saints—but he was bored and desperate. While he read those stories, something marvelous happened to him. As he thought about the heroic deeds of the saints, he thought to himself, *Hey! I can do that.* And he did! His name was Ignatius Loyola. He became a penitent, then a mystic, later a pilgrim, and finally a priest and founder of the Society of Jesus, whose members are called Jesuits. He is one of the most influential figures in church history, and it all started with a bored young patient who had nothing to read but some lives of saints. He wasn't the first person to find inspiration in the lives of holy men and women, and he wasn't the last.

Today we pay honor to all the saints. We don't want to leave any of them out, so we have a feast to include all of them. Many of them have been canonized and beatified, formally recognized as persons who achieved heroic sanctity. There are many, many more, of course, numerous beyond our imagining. They are unknown soldiers of Christ whose names are known only to God. Some of them are probably people we have known personally, folks we looked up to and admired in their lifetime. Saints come in all sizes and shapes. They are rich and poor, old and young, married and single, rulers and subjects, scholars and blue-collar workers, monks and hermits, clergy and lay, famous and obscure.

What they all had in common was that, one way or another, they fit the description of the men and women Jesus describes in today's gospel. In their hunger and thirst for righteousness, they were peacemakers, merciful, poor in spirit, sometimes persecuted, always clean of heart. We pray to them to intercede for us at the throne of God. Like Ignatius, we look to them for inspiration. And we have good reason to hope that, one day, we will be among their number, enjoying the vision of God in the fullness of life that he won for them and for us.

*What saint—canonized or not—has been a particular inspiration for you?*

## Immaculate Conception Celebrated on December 8

Gen 9:3–15, 20; Eph 1:3–6, 11–12; Luke 1:26–38

*Hail, full of grace! The Lord is with you.*

In a big football game several years ago, a player made a spectacular catch of a pass. A sportswriter who was running out of adjectives called it the "immaculate reception." As time went on, most fans have forgotten the origin of the phrase, but we know that it's a playful variation on the name of today's feast, the Immaculate Conception of our Lady, the Mother of God. But even some Catholics are confused about what we are celebrating today.

The doctrine of the immaculate conception of Mary is sometimes confused with another doctrine, that of the virgin birth. What adds to the confusion is the fact that the gospel reading is about the conception of Jesus, not of Mary. Since Mary was a virgin and conceived Jesus by the power of the

Holy Spirit, his coming into the world is called a virgin birth. But today's feast declares that, from the first moment of her existence, Mary was free from sin. We believe that, since God chose Mary to be the mother of his Son, he wanted her to be "full of grace." The feast is really not about conception itself, but about Mary being graced.

When we say that Mary was always free from sin, what are we talking about? She led an ordinary, workaday life like all of us. She and Joseph must have experienced the strains and annoyances that go with married life. She must have yelled at the boy Jesus when he left his room a mess and she had to pick up after him. Sin is a turning away from God, a loss of direction in our lives, and there was none of that in her life. She was always attuned to God's will and living out her vocation to holiness.

This great privilege was bestowed on Mary not for her sake but because she was chosen to participate in the work of salvation. We, too, are called to make our contribution to the saving work of our Lord. Redemption comes to all of us, Mary included, from Jesus; and Jesus comes to us through Mary. This feast comes at a good time of year. It is a prelude to Christmas, which is coming in a few weeks. Today we celebrate the mother of us all, and a life lived in the fullness of grace and the love of God.

*How does this feast help me to draw close to Mary?*